Bible Answers 101

Bruce BICKEL
&
Stan JANTZ

HARVEST HOUSE PUBLISHERS

EUGENE, OREGON

Cover by Left Coast Design, Portland, Oregon

Cover illustration © Krieg Barrie Illustration

CHRISTIANITY 101 is a registered trademark of Bruce Bickel and Stan Jantz. Harvest House Publishers, Inc., is the exclusive licensee of the federally registered trademark CHRISTIANITY 101.

BIBLE ANSWERS 101

Copyright © 2006 by Bruce Bickel and Stan Jantz
Published by Harvest House Publishers
Eugene, Oregon 97402
www.harvesthousepublishers.com

Library of Congress Cataloging-in-Publication Data
Bickel, Bruce, 1952-
  [Bible answers to life's big questions]
  Bible answers 101 / Bruce Bickel and Stan Jantz.
      p. cm. — (Christianity 101)
  Originally published: Bible answers to life's big questions, c2006.
  ISBN 978-0-7369-2525-9 (pbk.)
  1. Bible—Miscellanea. 2. Christian life—Biblical teaching. I. Jantz, Stan, 1952- II. Title. III. Title:
Bible answers one hundred one. IV. Title: Bible answers one hundred and one.
  BS612.B53 2009
  230'.041--dc22
                                    2008032938

Printed in the United States of America

        09   10   11   12   13   14   15   / BP-MS /   10   9   8   7   6   5   4   3   2   1

Contents

Be Careful
What You Ask For

*B*e careful what you ask for." No doubt you have heard that expression, and perhaps you have experienced the results of asking for something, only to be completely unprepared for the answer. Ten years ago, when we wrote the first of a series of books about God, the Bible, and various aspects of the Christian life, we asked our readers to send us e-mails with their questions about the topics in our book. E-mail technology was pretty new back then, so we didn't know A) how many people out there even used e-mail or B) how many people would take the time to respond.

Well, as the saying goes, we asked for it, and we got it—lots of e-mails with lots of questions. Not only did readers respond, but they also posed the kinds of questions you might expect to ask someone like Dr. Phil or Dr. Dobson. They were real-life questions from real people filled with concern, confusion, and just plain old curiosity. From the very beginning we personally answered each question sent to us, a practice that has not stopped after ten years, many books, and more than ten thousand e-mails.

If we had known then what we know now, we may not have asked for questions in that first book and all the books that followed. Not because we don't like hearing from our readers—that's what makes writing books worthwhile—but because we have often wondered if we're qualified to answer them. We're not Dr. Dobson or Dr. Phil or Dr. Anybody, so we've wondered at times if we're in over our heads.

Actually, that's not a bad place to be. When it comes to God and what He wants for us, we need to feel that we're in over our heads because that's precisely when God can use us. Jesus once told the apostle Paul, "My gracious favor is all you need. My power works best in your weakness" (2 Corinthians 12:9). If we believe we can do something in our own strength and with our own knowledge, we're not going to get very far. But when we admit we are weak and don't know everything, God will step up and give us the power and understanding we need. That's why Paul writes, "For I can do everything with the help of Christ who gives me the strength I need" (Philippians 4:13). This is the way we approach each of the questions people ask us. We rely on Christ's strength—and His Word—to help us give the best possible answer.

The book you are holding contains just a small percentage of the questions we have received over the years, but they are the questions that best represent the topics and the issues people wonder about most. To the best of our ability—and in the strength of Christ—we have tried to give Bible answers. You may not agree with every answer we have given, but we think you will be stimulated in your own study of God's Word. And who knows, you may also be encouraged along the way.

We also think you will identify with many of the questions because they come from people just like you who desire to grow in their faith but nonetheless have sincere doubts about certain aspects of the Christian life. For the sake of privacy, we have withheld any names, but you can be assured that these are the kind of real people you would feel quite comfortable with over a cup of coffee. In fact, that's how we are picturing you, sitting across the table, perhaps in a Starbucks (our favorite hangout), discussing things that really matter.

Oh, and by the way, if you have a question of your own, we want you to know that we're not done answering our e-mails. Far from it. We will continue to answer every question sent to us. So, if you've got one, write to us at info@christianity101online.com.

If you don't have a question but just want to learn more about us and the books we write, check out our website at www.christianity101online.com.

One more thing. Since this book is based on Bible answers, we want to give you a verse from the Bible that we've included in just about every book we have ever written. We like it because it comes from God Himself, who makes this promise:

> *"For I know the plans I have for you," says the* LORD. *"They are plans for good and not for disaster, to give you a future and a hope. In those days when you pray, I will listen. If you look for me in earnest, you will find me when you seek me. I will be found by you," says the* LORD (Jeremiah 29:11-14).

Chapter 1
God

*M*any people told us that they believe in the existence of God, but they wonder about His character. What is He like? Is He detached from the world He created, or is He a micromanager in the details of our lives? It is easy to conceptualize God when staring into space or looking at a majestic sunrise. But how can God allow the tragedies that exist on earth? These are honest questions.

How can we find God?
I am really trying to find God. How do I know when I have found Him? I started searching about four years ago, and I'm still not sure if God knows I exist. Any insight would be helpful. Thanks.

Thanks so much for your e-mail and your honest question about finding God. You have been persistent in your search. Let's see if we can give you some insights.

First of all, here's a promise from God Himself: "If you look for me in earnest, you will find me when you seek me. I will be found by you" (Jeremiah 29:13-14).

Sometimes people wonder why God hasn't revealed Himself more directly than He has. We can't explain that except to say that many things about God are mysteries. If we could figure everything out about God, would He still be God or merely some human invention?

Here's what God says about Himself: "'My thoughts are completely different from yours,' says the LORD. 'And my ways are far beyond anything you could imagine. For just as the heavens are higher than the earth, so are my ways higher than your ways and my thoughts higher than your thoughts'" (Isaiah 55:8-9).

So we have to realize and accept the fact that God is very different from us, and we can't know Him like we might know another human being. Yet we can know God, and we can know about Him by accessing the clear and definitive clues He has left for us.

These clues are objective; they are testable. In fact, as you study Christianity and compare it to other religions, you will find that it is the only "testable" religion. It can be tested according to history, archaeology, science, and reason. (You can't test everything, of course, but you can test enough to give you a high degree of certainty that Christianity is true.)

But don't forget about the element of faith. God wants you to put your faith and trust in His promise to reveal Himself to you. As Almighty God of the universe, He could make His existence and presence painfully obvious to everyone, and He could force our allegiance and worship. Or He could buy our love and loyalty by blessing us with health and prosperity as long as we obeyed Him. But that is not how God operates. He wants our obedience and worship to be motivated by a reverential love for Him. We voluntarily believe what we have not yet seen.

Even Christians in New Testament times had to believe in things they couldn't see. The apostle Paul explained, "So we don't look at the troubles we can see right now; rather, we look forward to what we have not yet seen. For the troubles we see will soon be over, but the joys to come will last forever" (2 Corinthians 4:18). He later added, "We live by believing and not by seeing" (2 Corinthians 5:7).

We are accustomed to living in a world where we believe something only after we have seen it. With Christianity, we will see after we have first believed. When the apostle Thomas had a hard time with this, Jesus Himself said, "Blessed are those who haven't seen me and believe anyway" (John 20:29).

We know that God is aware of your existence; He already loves you. He is anxious to reveal Himself to you.

Did God create evil?
Recently I read your book *Knowing God 101,* and I have to ask you a question pertaining to something you said. You state that Satan was a created angel, and then you go on to say that God is incapable of creating evil. Therefore, Satan was created without evil. He became evil of his own free will. This doesn't make sense. God created Satan, so God had to create evil. Otherwise, how could evil come to be, even if we do have free will? The evil had to be there to begin with. Maybe you could elaborate on this topic further.

Theologians and philosophers have wrestled with this question for centuries. It's one of the big questions of the ages. The question is either phrased as, "How could a loving God allow evil?" or, as you are phrasing it, "How could a holy God create evil?"

The first question is perhaps a bit easier to answer. The reason a loving God allows evil—or anything that comes short of His perfect standard for that matter—is that if He didn't allow evil and sin, we would all be destroyed because all of us are sinners. We all fall short of God's perfect standard (Romans 6:23). He allows us to exist, even as sinful creatures, because He loves us. The Bible tells us that God will judge evil someday. Meanwhile, He is being patient, giving more time for people to turn to Him (2 Peter 3:8-9).

The second question—the one you're concerned with—is a bit tougher. You are asserting that God had to create evil; if He didn't, it wouldn't exist. Let's look at this from a couple of perspectives.

One viewpoint approaches the issue by assuming that God is what He creates. To assert that God created evil would mean that He is evil. If this is true, then God would no longer be holy. But God's holiness precludes Him from having any connection with sin. "God's holiness denotes not merely His separation from sin in the perfection of His own being, but His abhorrence of it and hostility to it" (A.S. Wood). In the presence of God's holiness, humankind becomes aware of its sin (Isaiah 6:3-8). Holiness is not merely one of God's attributes (such as the fact that He is all-powerful). It represents His essential nature. So if we say God created evil, then He is no longer holy. He is no longer God.

Another viewpoint focuses on the creation—that which God creates, be it angels, humanity, or the material universe. God could have created all beings and the universe without the capability of doing wrong, or of choosing wrong. But what good would that have been? If someone loves you, would you feel differently if that person loved you only because he or she had no choice in the matter? Of course you would. God is no different. He didn't want beings who loved Him because they had no choice. He wanted beings who loved Him voluntarily, or of their own free will. So He created angels and humanity with the capacity to choose to love Him or not and to obey Him or not.

God created a perfect world, but it was a world full of choices. In fact, you could say that by creating it that way, He demonstrated His love and perfection. Had God created a world in which all creatures were obligated to obey and love, one could make the case that God did not create a perfect world, at least not by the standards of perfection as we would understand them.

Creating beings with the capacity to sin is not the same as creating sin. To use an analogy, let's say that a dad made a baseball bat out of a tree branch so his son could play baseball. But then someone stole the bat and used it to kill someone. Does that mean that the dad created a murder weapon? Even more, does it mean that the dad is responsible for causing the murder? Of course not. Our legal system recognizes the difference between the person who makes something for a good purpose and someone who uses that object to commit an evil act. The flaw is not with the maker but with the one who choses to commit the evil.

God created Satan and the fallen angels for good, but they made their choice to turn that good into evil. The same goes for humanity. The difference between angels and humanity is that the angels have no chance for redemption, but we humans do. We have the opportunity to be made righteous, or perfect, through the perfect and sacrificial life of Jesus Christ. The love of God intervenes despite our sin.

Perhaps we took this further than you wanted. If so, we apologize! But we hope you can see our point. If not, let us know! Thanks again for writing, and thanks for reading *Knowing God 101.*

Why does God allow children to suffer?

I am a chaplain in a prison, and recently an inmate asked me why God allows people to harm children. I explained to him that God doesn't allow these things. We are all sinners, and sadly, some are worse than others. The people that commit these tragic crimes make the choice to do so. Our free will allows us to make choices, and unfortunately, some people make choices that are terrible. He has now asked why God allows children to die in natural disasters when this is clearly not the choice of man. I'm sorry to say that this has me stumped. Could you please help me with an answer for him and for myself?

The whole issue of God allowing evil is a tough one. It takes a lot of thought—and prayer—to even begin to understand how a loving and holy God can allow the tragedies of child abuse and other horrors.

First, we need to understand that God does allow evil. If you didn't believe that He allowed evil, then you would have to believe that He is powerless to stop it when it happens. And we know that isn't true. As the sovereign, all-powerful God and Creator of the universe, God allows everything. Nothing good—or bad—happens outside of His control. But this is different from God initiating and causing the evil and suffering. As a holy and perfect God, He is incapable of evil, and He cannot cause evil.

Let's look at this another way. If God did not allow evil, He would have to destroy everything that is evil, including us (by that we mean all of humanity, not just Bruce and Stan). But in His great love and mercy, God not only allows us to live, but He has given us a way to get back into a right relationship with Him. (Read Romans 5:5-11.)

Even though God allows evil now, that doesn't mean He will allow it forever. The Scripture is clear that right now, God is being patient with us so that more people will repent. But His judgment of sin will come. (Read 2 Peter 3:8-10.)

Just as sin has infected the human race (such that we cause evil not intended by God), so the natural world is under the curse of sin, sometimes causing terrible disasters. In general, our world operates in marvelous ways. Simply by looking at the wonder of God's creation, we can see the glory of God (Psalm 19). At the same time, creation isn't perfect. Scripture says, "Against its will, everything on earth was subjected to God's curse. All creation anticipates the day when it will join God's children in glorious freedom from death and decay. For we know that all creation has been groaning as in the pains of childbirth right up to the present time" (Romans 8:20-22).

Just as the earth groans under the weight of sin, most people groan in shock, dismay, and disgust at child abuse. But that is the effect of sin. Still, we can be confident that it will come to an end in God's timing.

Why do bad things happen?
I work with someone who doesn't really believe in God. His wife's sister was murdered a while ago, and he says, "If God has all the power in the world, why do bad things happen?" I am not really sure how to respond to him, to make him see that it is not God's doing, that it is because of sin. Also, how can I get him to open his eyes to Christ?

The question about how an all-powerful and all-loving God can allow suffering and evil is legitimate. Christians should be glad whenever people ask them this question because the people presenting the question are thinking about God. Of course, Christians should be prepared to answer it. Unfortunately, the answer requires some thought.

The question of God and evil goes to the heart of free will. God created humanity with the capacity to choose between right and wrong. That's all well and good, but this freedom has a drawback. If we choose evil, then all kinds of bad things happen, as your friend at work has experienced.

But what's the alternative? If evil did not exist, we would not have free will. We would be creatures with no choice but to do good. All of us—including your friend—would be required to bow down to God through no choice of our own. Because God wants us to love Him willingly, He isn't going to force us to choose Him or to do what is right in all circumstances. Thus, evil exists because God loved us enough to give us freedom of choice.

Your friend might logically ask, "Even though God didn't initiate evil, why doesn't He do something to stop it once it happens?" God is going to do something about it— that's what judgment is all about. (When that happens, only those who have willingly chosen God by receiving Jesus will escape eternal judgment.) Yes, God is going to deal with evil, but that means He'll be dealing with us.

But again, because of God's love for us, He hasn't fully implemented eternal judgment yet for one simple reason. Here it is in 2 Peter 3:9-10:

> The Lord isn't really being slow about his promise to return, as some people think. No, he is being patient for your sake. He does not want anyone to perish, so he is giving more time for everyone to repent. But the day of the Lord will come as unexpectedly as a thief. Then the heavens will pass away with a terrible noise, and everything in them

will disappear in fire, and the earth and everything
on it will be exposed to judgment.

Your friend at work is free to believe or not believe in God, but that doesn't change who God is. The other thing to think about is this: If there's no God, what's the alternative? The alternative is that we still have evil, but in the end there's no hope. When death happens, that's it. Game over. Nothing. But with God in the picture, we have hope. Hope that one day God will deal with evil, and we will spend eternity with God in absolute glory and perfection, with no evil and no suffering and no pain (Revelation 21:3-4).

The real question your friend should be asking is whether he or she has enough reason to believe that God doesn't exist. The argument that evil is in the world isn't a very good reason (although people frequently use it as a smoke screen so that they don't have to deal with the ultimate question).

Pray and ask God for wisdom as you talk with your friend. God has put you in a strategic position. Stay connected with your friend and let your light shine so that the presence of Jesus will be on display. Don't condemn honest questions about God, but simply recommend the life of faith in Jesus that you have chosen. Ask God to work through your answers and your life, and ask Him to open your friend's heart to His message. And be patient. God will work through you in His time.

? What is the correct view of the Trinity?
The concept of the Trinity is hard to understand. I'm not sure if I'm on the right track. Here's what I think of the Trinity. God the Father, God the Son, and God the Holy Spirit existed as three separate Gods in heaven. God created the universe first, and then Adam and Eve's sin

brought sin and hell to our life, so Jesus was sent by God as a human to the world to redeem our sins and burdens. The very day that He went back to heaven as God after He was resurrected, Jesus Christ sent the Holy Spirit down to help us connect with Him and other brothers and sisters on earth. We may use Jesus Christ as a way of getting to know God the Father, who is the Creator of the universe. Please advise if there is anything wrong with my understanding.

You are right, the concept of the Trinity is difficult to understand, but there is a way to start out on the right track. Unfortunately, you aren't on that track!

God is one God (Isaiah 45:5). Believing in three separate Gods is called polytheism. Christianity is based on the biblical doctrine of monotheism.

God is one God in three Persons—God the Father, God the Son, and God the Holy Spirit. All three possess the qualities of God, and all three are distinct Persons, but they are not separate Gods. Again, the correct doctrine (teaching) starts with one God in three Persons. This is called Tri-unity. God is a triune God. The idea of tri-Gods (as you put it) is polytheism.

All three members of the Trinity have existed eternally. All three were involved in creation. Yes, God sent Jesus to earth. Jesus is God in the flesh. As Jesus told His disciples, "Anyone who has seen me has seen the Father...Don't you believe that I am in the Father and the Father is in me?" (John 14:9-10).

You're to be congratulated that you're thinking about this difficult concept. Keep with it.

How do we know the Trinity exists?

I'm dealing with someone who says that the Trinity doesn't exist. He says that the "Father," "Son," and "Holy Spirit" references are just references to the same God. He says it is like calling God by the names "Lord," "Heavenly Father," and "Almighty God." This doesn't sound right to me, but I'm not sure how to respond to him. Are there any passages in the Bible that could help me argue with him?

We'll be glad to give you some Bible references, but not simply for the sake of helping you win an argument. A correct understanding of the Trinity is important for your growth as a Christian (and for your friend's understanding of God).

Several times in the Bible we find the presence of all three members of the Godhead mentioned simultaneously:

- The Trinity is referenced in the work of Creation ("Let us make people in our image"—Genesis 1:26-27).

- We see the Trinity at the baptism of Jesus (with the voice of God the Father and the Holy Spirit descending as a dove—Matthew 3:16-17).

- Jesus Himself made reference to the three members of the Trinity when He told His disciples to "make disciples of all the nations, baptizing them in the name of the Father and the Son and the Holy Spirit"—(Matthew 28:19).

- The apostle Paul gave a benediction that acknowledges the Trinity (see 2 Corinthians 13:13).

In these passages you have the Bible referring to the three separate Persons of the Trinity. The "Father, Son, and

Holy Spirit" references are clearly not interchangeable nick-names for the same entity.

Some people have tried to describe the Trinity with various analogies, such as a father (who is also a son and a husband), an apple (skin, meat, and core), an egg (shell, white, and yoke), and water (steam, liquid, and ice). At first glance these analogies seem to fit, but they fail under correct theological scrutiny.

Let's take the father-son-husband analogy and see why it falls short. (In face, it's heresy.) The Trinity is three distinct Persons in one being, and each one is fully God. Yet there is only one God, not three Gods. The problem with the father-son-husband analogy is that it describes one person—a man—who is engaged in three different family roles. That isn't the Trinity. It's an ancient heresy called modalism, which teaches that God simply exists in three different modes. That isn't the orthodox, historic teaching of the Christian church.

God is one being, but He exists in three Persons: Father, Son, and Holy Spirit. A man is one being and one person who may have three different roles. God is three Persons in one being. Three identities is not the same as three Persons. God has always existed eternally in three distinct Persons, yet He is one being. This is central to the doctrine of the Trinity.

Does this blow your mind? It did ours. We've given up trying to identify an analogy for the Trinity. We don't think there is an adequate analogy to anything we know of here in the natural world. Maybe that shouldn't surprise us since the Trinity is supernatural.

How can we respond to an atheist?

I have a 15-year-old nephew who does not believe God exists. Can you please help me? I need your advice on how I can assist this young man, show him a way out of his atheism, and bring him to believe in God.

You have reason to be concerned about your nephew, but don't worry that he is an atheist. Young people this age normally have questions about serious issues, and God (and His existence) is often near the top of the list. He may not believe in God, but that doesn't mean he has good reasons to support his belief. Maybe he's upset at something, or perhaps he's being influenced by a friend. In any case, his "belief" probably doesn't mean he has thought the whole thing through and has concluded God doesn't exist.

Our best advice is to just be open to listen to your nephew. If he will talk with you, let him talk. Ask him to explain how he arrived at his belief. Resist the temptation to straighten him out or to "bring him to believe in God." Make clear that this is something that he'll have to decide for himself but that you're curious to know the basis for his belief and conclusions. He may just want someone to talk to but nobody will listen, so he's making a rather outlandish statement to evoke reactions.

If you listen and then respond with statements such as, "It seems to me…" or "I have found in my experience and study…" he may be much more likely to hear what you are saying. Don't react in a big way, such as saying, "What do you mean you don't believe in God! Are you nuts! You're on a fast track to hell, Bucko, unless you get your head screwed on straight." Of course, you aren't going to respond like that, but we're all tempted to overreact when the spiritual destiny of people we love is at stake. That usually doesn't get us very far.

For yourself, you may want to do a little preparation. Most Christians aren't very comfortable explaining the existence of God, not because they don't believe but because they don't feel adequately prepared. You may want to check out our book *Knowing God 101,* which covers the basics on the issue of God's existence, His character, and so forth.

Finally, don't forget to pray for your nephew. Ask God to give you opportunities to talk, and ask God to give your nephew an open heart.

? How can we help an agnostic?

I hope you can help me. My son has become an agnostic. I would like to bring him back into God's reach, but I'm not sure how. Every time I bring up the subject we get into an argument. I pray for him and hope that he will see the light, but I'm just not sure what else to do. He's had a tough time in his life. He's only 27 but has lived a lot. He had a drug problem in his teens and until he was about 23. He got himself off of them. He also has hepatitis (from the drugs). I try telling him prayer will help, but it hasn't done any good. (I've had breast cancer and feel prayer is what got me through it.) When we do actually talk about God, he says he's not sure what he believes, and he doubts that one entity controls everything. Can you help me in any way to help my son?

Our hearts go out to you regarding your son, but you are not without hope. Honestly, a young man like your son who has made some unfortunate choices is likely to feel as if he can't know God. As you know, that's the primary definition of an agnostic—someone who doesn't think God is knowable. (By contrast, an atheist doesn't think God exists.)

So an agnostic at least acknowledges the potential existence of God, but through various circumstances or lack of information, he doesn't think God can be known.

The fact that your son doesn't believe that one entity can control everything just shows that he hasn't thought his position through enough. That's okay. Don't push him.

However, you can challenge him to think his position through to its logical conclusion. Is he a reader? If so, you can suggest a good book, such as *A Case for Christ* by Lee Strobel or *More Than a Carpenter* by Josh McDowell, which is a bit simpler.

If he isn't open to getting more information on his own, you can simply talk with him (which means you may need to do some reading yourself). Don't press but ask questions. Ask him how he has come to his conclusions. Share with him how prayer has made a difference in your life, especially when you were facing your own life-threatening illness.

And continue to pray. God is faithful. He doesn't always answer in the manner and in the time that we would like, but His timing is always perfect.

Christiainity: exclusive or inclusive?
In your Bible study on Ephesians, you state that Christianity is both exclusive and inclusive. These seem contradictory. What Scripture supports this idea?

Christianity is exclusive in the sense that it provides only one way to get right with God (see John 14:6 and Acts 4:12), and Jesus Christ is the exclusive path to God. Some people interpret that "one way to God" as intolerance on the part of Christianity. But in reality, Christianity is inclusive because a relationship with Christ is available to everyone. A person can be male or female, rich or poor, Jew or Gentile, slave or free...anyone can come to Christ Jesus (see Galatians 3:27-28).

Where did God come from?
Where did God come from? If you say He always was and always will be, you're not really answering the question.

Where did God come from? is an excellent and difficult question. The answer is based on both logic and faith.

First, the logic. Everything that exists must have a cause. Nothing comes from nothing. But does that mean God has a cause? No, if God had a cause, He would not be God. By definition, God is uncaused because an endless string of causes would be impossible. At some point a first cause must have gotten all the other causes going. The best explanation for this first cause is God, who by definition is uncaused.

This rule applies to the universe itself. Science now believes that the universe had a beginning, sometimes referred to as the Big Bang. The question is, where did the Big Bang come from? The only logical answer is that it was initiated by the first cause.

So what or who is the first cause? This is where faith comes in. You could simply believe that the first cause is an impersonal entity that is completely detached from the universe, or you could believe that the first cause is personal and has communicated with the created world in some way. No one can scientifically prove that the first cause is personal and communicative, but God has given us evidence. It's up to you to investigate.

Why would God create people destined for hell?

I have a friend who grew up going to Catholic school but now rejects almost everything about God. Her problem with Christianity is this: Why would God knowingly create people who are destined for hell? How do I respond to her?

Ask your friend why she thinks people are destined for hell. Show her from the Bible that anyone who believes in

Jesus Christ will not perish but will have everlasting life (John 3:16). Tell her that God doesn't want anyone to die an eternal death (2 Peter 3:9).

No person is destined for hell unless he or she chooses to go there by refusing Christ.

God loves us, and He wants us to be restored to a relationship with Him. Sin has broken that relationship, but we can get back into a right relationship with God. The Bible says, "The wages of sin is death, but the free gift of God is eternal life through Jesus Christ our Lord" (Romans 6:23).

Is it okay to ask God questions?
Do you think asking God questions and doubting God's sovereignty and faithfulness are synonymous?

They are not the same. Asking God questions is perfectly reasonable even though we may not always get the answers (at least not the answers we like). You can ask God through prayer, by studying His Word, and by talking with mature believers. On the other hand, doubting God's sovereignty and faithfulness is the same as doubting God's omnipotence and His truthfulness. In other words, asking questions of God is one thing; questioning God's character is quite another. Of course, one of your questions may be, "God, why did You fail me?" or "God, why do You allow suffering in the world?" It's okay to ask these questions because they have reasonable answers. But to say that God is unable to help you or powerless to prevent suffering would be the same as questioning His sovereignty and faithfulness.

Should I care whether or not God exists?
I'm 13, and I really need some help. I don't know if I should really care about all this God stuff or if He

really exists, and I don't know if I should feel anything special to know that God is in my life. Please help if it is not too much trouble.

Those are great questions to be asking. Many adults skip over them, so we're glad you're thinking about them. We happen to think thinking about God is very important. In fact, you can't help it. Everybody thinks about God in one way or another. Even people who don't think God exists think about God, which should tell you something.

You can't prove God exists the way you can prove that a chair or a dog or a person exists, because you can actually touch and see the chair, the dog, and the person. But you can know God exists based on the evidence in the universe. Here are three simple pieces of evidence for the existence of God:

1. The very fact that you and everybody else thinks about God points to His existence. If you were the only person who thought about God, then we could just say that you have an imaginary friend. But everyone thinks about God. That's more than just a coincidence.

2. Everything in the universe has a cause. If something doesn't have a cause, it doesn't exist. But what caused the causes? In other words, when you go back in the string of causes, there must have been a first cause to get all of the other causes going. An infinite string of causes would be impossible. And the first cause must itself not be caused. It must have preexisted. It is reasonable to believe that the first cause is God, who has always existed.

3. The universe and everything in it has amazing order, harmony, purpose, and design. If you saw a beautiful Ferrari sitting in your driveway, would you assume that it just appeared out of nowhere, or would you believe someone put it there? Would you believe that all of the parts and pieces assembled themselves, or would you believe that someone designed and built the car? The same is true with the universe. Everything is so fine-tuned for life that an intelligent designer must have been behind it all. You can't explain creation from random mutation or chance.

So what difference does God make in your life? Well, if God created the universe and everything in it, then He created you. Wouldn't you think that He did it for a reason? Don't you want to know if He had a reason? And if so, don't you what to know the reason?

You'll need to come to some decisions on your own, but let us give you a head start. We believe that God created you, that He knows you, and that He loves you. You aren't some uncreated, uncaused blob of tissue who came from nothing and is going nowhere. You are a significant human being created by God. You have a purpose that includes being in a personal relationship with God. That's why you should care about all of this God stuff.

Why should we fear God?

I don't understand why the first step in Christianity should be based on the fear of God. Why should I fear God, when I know He loves me more than anyone else ever could? He gives me everything I need. I am trying to learn more about the Bible, but I can't find this explained anywhere in my books or Bibles. Maybe you can explain it to me. I know God is the most powerful being and that what He says, He will do, but I'm not afraid of Him. Should I be? Thank you, and I love your book *Knowing the Bible 101.*

The fear of God is actually an important part of the Christian life, but we think you misunderstand the terminology.

We like Chuck Swindoll's definition best: "To fear God means to take Him seriously and do what He says."

Fearing God has nothing to do with being afraid of God. The essence of God is love, not fear (1 John 4:8-10,18). The Bible always connects the fear of God with blessing. When we obey God and seek His will, we are doing what He says. You could say we are fearing God.

But always remember that love was what motivated God to save you, and the love of God will always be with you. But God is holy, and sin will always be an offense to Him. At the same time, His love isn't based on what you do but on what Jesus already did for you by dying for your sins. That's what John 3:16 is all about.

What is the right way to worship God?

In John 4:23-24, Jesus tells us that God is looking for people who will worship Him "in spirit and in truth." I'm not sure what that means.

Worshipping God in Spirit means recognizing that He is a Spirit and not a physical being confined to one place. God is omnipresent (present everywhere all the time), and He can be worshipped anywhere and at any time. This doesn't mean you look at a rock and worship God in the rock. God is not the rock; He is not the physical universe. (That is pantheism.) God is *transcendent* (that is, apart from us and our physical reality), yet He is *immanent* (that is, near to us in every way). Worshipping God in truth means worshipping the one true God, not some idea we have about God that is based on our personal conceptions rather than how the Bible describes God.

> **? Is it possible to not believe in God?**
> Do you believe people are for real when they say they don't believe in God? I think they are lying, and deep down they know they are lying. What do you think?

When dealing with people, you should take them at their word, at least as a starting point. In our Christianity 101 book entitled *World Religions & Cults 101,* we devote an entire chapter to the atheistic worldview (also known as naturalism). We talk about two kinds of atheists.

The "weak position" atheists say they don't believe in God because no one has provided any credible evidence that God exists. They want the burden of proof shifted to the theists. No one can categorically prove that God exists (you can't reduce God to a science experiment), but plenty of reasonable evidence points to His existence (as we discussed in *Knowing God 101*).

The other kind of atheist is the "strong position" atheist. This atheist firmly believes that God does not exist. Here, the burden of proof is on the atheist to prove there is no God, and that's not easy. More reasonable proof—from logic, science, history, and anthropology—points to God's existence than to His nonexistence.

Now, you asked a very basic question, and for that we can give you a pretty direct answer. Do atheists really believe that God doesn't exist, or are they choosing that position so they can live their lives the way they want? We think you're right that they have to enter into a kind of self-deception, and here's why. Read Romans 1:18-20. Clearly the God of creation has made Himself known to His created beings. He has put the knowledge about Himself in every human heart. Whether someone admits that or not, the knowledge is there.

A reasonable person might wonder why the atheists spend so much time thinking about God if He doesn't exist.

Why should we suffer for Adam's sin?

Let's say I was a perfect, righteous, and sinless father. And let's say I had a son, and I told him that when he gets of age (let's say 15), he will not be allowed to commit any sin or be tricked into sinning by anything. He must be perfect like his father. So of course, the boy sins by age 15 and one month. When I find out, I come back and punish him by putting him in jail for life, but I don't stop there; I also make all of his kids and their kids and every generation of his seed go to jail upon birth. My question to you is this: Do you feel that the curse of all humanity because of Adam is honestly fair? I know God is perfect in all His decisions, but I just have a hard time accepting this "one strike and you're out" godly standard. What do you guys think?

We really admire the way you are wrestling with these issues of sin and God's fairness. You are a thoughtful person who desires to understand God and the way He works in our world and in our lives.

This issue isn't easy. It's probably the toughest issue of all, and many people reject God altogether because they can't reconcile it. You seek to understand while trusting God to do the right thing. This is such a healthy approach.

Centuries ago Anselm of Canterbury wrote, "I believe so that I may understand." When you trust God by faith that He has saved you through the life, the death, and the resurrection of Christ, you receive the gift of forgiveness and the promise of eternal life.

At the same time, your belief must lead to understanding—perhaps not a complete understanding, but a growing understanding in the person and the ways of our great God. Most people don't take the journey to understanding that you are on. What a shame! Without the struggle and the reward of learning to know God better, our lives here on earth are so shallow.

Your illustration is an excellent one, but it doesn't capture the absolute holiness of God. When we put ourselves in God's place, we bring Him to our level. In other words, your illustration assumes that God would think the way we do (it's called *anthropomorphizing* God). We think He should behave the way we would or the way we would like Him to.

Of course, you would have compassion on your own 15-year-old son. A father who condemned a son after one offense would be considered an unfit father. In fact, you would give your son a second and third and fourth chance. You would probably give him all the chances in the world.

But God is not us. He is God, and apart from Him there is no other. When He created humankind, He did so in His own image. He created us as sinless people but with the capacity to sin. He created us so that we could willingly love Him. With that choice came the capacity to sin. God clearly explained what would happen if humanity sinned. And He made the penalty harsh because of the nature of sin. Sin is so offensive to God that He cannot even be in the presence of sin. The very word "holy" means to be set apart from sin.

If you don't mind, let's take your illustration and modify it a bit. Let's say a judge tells someone who has never committed a crime, "If you ever commit murder, I'm going to bring you before this court and pronounce a death sentence. If you don't, you can live your life freely and without penalty. In fact, I'll even keep in contact with you. We can have lunch occasionally and develop a personal relationship."

Then, let's say this person goes out and defied the judge's order and murders someone. At first he tries to hide his crime, but the judge knows and quickly calls the offender before his bench. What do you think the judge should do? Should the judge say, "You know, that thing I said about giving you the death penalty, well, that was really more like a warning. It was just a suggestion. I know people make mistakes, so I'm going to give you another chance. Just don't go out and murder someone else."

Would you consider that justice? Would it have been unjust for the judge to tell the offender, "I told you exactly what would happen, and yet you went out and murdered anyway. Because you have violated my directive, I'm going to impose the sentence"? Of course not. But that's not where the story ends. Let's say the judge then told the offender, "The death sentence cannot be changed, but I love you. In fact, I love you so much that I'm going to take your penalty and give it to someone else, someone who has volunteered to die in your place. I've agreed to accept this substitute, not because of you, but because of the volunteer. Oh, by the way, this volunteer happens to be my only son."

That sounds preposterous, doesn't it? Yet that's exactly what God has done for us. It's the story of God. It's the story of His great love for us—the very people who have offended Him and violated His standard.

The Bible says, "But God showed his great love for us by sending Christ to die for us while we were still sinners" (Romans 5:8).

God bless you as you come to grips with the awesome love of God!

Chapter 2
Jesus

Even though more people follow Jesus than any other religious figure, many people have questions about the central figure of the Christian faith. Who was Jesus, and why was He sent to earth? How could Jesus be fully God and fully man? And perhaps the most perplexing question for many of our readers is this: How can Jesus be the only way to God? Read on as we answer those questions and more.

Are there contradictions in the Gospels?

I have been a Christian for about eight years now (previously an atheist), and it's been an amazing journey. I have been growing and stumbling through my new life, learning all I can and always yearning for more. Recently, while studying the Gospels, I became alarmed at the contradictions concerning the events at the empty tomb. I would think that of any event in Jesus' life, this would be the most important—that He indeed rose from the dead, that His tomb wasn't tampered with or some other explanation for His disappearance. How could the Gospel accounts be so different? If we are to believe these men, how could they get their stories wrong? Is someone lying? If God is the author of the

Bible, how could He let this happen? I believe by faith, and my experiences are very real, but still this bothers me. For someone not of faith, I would think this would ruin the credibility of the story of Jesus. If I didn't know any better, I would rethink Jesus as The One. Maybe the Jews have it right. What would I say to someone who is searching if they came to this? I just can't get my mind around this! Am I silly to make such a big deal? Thank you for reading this. I look forward to your reply.

Thanks for your e-mail and your questions about the resurrection. The notion that the Gospels contradict themselves with regard to the resurrection has been around for centuries, and it is easily answered. Each Gospel is like a biography written by an eyewitness. As each of the four eyewitnesses—Matthew, Mark, Luke, and John—wrote his account of what he saw, each one brought a little different perspective to the book he wrote, based to some degree on his own personality.

For example, let's say four different people witnessed a car accident involving a mom and a dad and two kids. The first eyewitness may comment on what kind of car was involved. The second person may not mention the car but instead focus on the conditions present at the time of the accident (the road was slippery or it was dark). The third eyewitness might observe that two adults were involved in the accident, while the fourth person might report that there was a family of four.

Each of these eyewitness observations does not match the others, and they could appear to be contradictory—especially the third account, which mentioned two adults, and the fourth account, which referred to a family of four. In fact, all four eyewitnesses are accurately reporting what they saw. Yes, two adults were involved, and yes, a family of four was involved in the accident. Just because the eyewitnesses don't report the same facts doesn't mean they contradict one another.

What you are doing—questioning the Scripture with an open mind—is entirely appropriate. God doesn't expect us to have blind faith. Our faith is rooted in evidence and substance. Hebrews 11:1-2 says, "What is faith? It is the confident assurance that what we hope for is going to happen. It is the evidence of things we cannot yet see."

God invites our questions, and He wants us to know what we believe. One time the apostle Paul, the greatest missionary the world has ever seen, came to the town of Berea. The people of Berea were skeptical of Paul, so they dug into Scripture to make sure what he was saying was accurate. Here's what Acts 17:11 says:

> And the people of Berea were more open-minded than those in Thessalonica, and they listened eagerly to Paul's message. They searched the Scriptures day after day to check up on Paul and Silas, to see if they were really teaching the truth.

So keep searching the Scriptures! God and His Word can stand the test of questions.

Does the Bible say we have to accept Jesus?
I'm trying to find Scripture that says you have to accept Jesus Christ as your Savior before you die. I know it is true, but until I see the Scripture, I can't accept it completely. Wait—that's not quite what I mean. What I mean is, how do I tell someone it's true if it isn't supported by the Scriptures? I believe it, but I have to be sure before I tell someone else.

You are very wise to verify an important truth like salvation from Scripture. Sometimes people will come up with an idea and say that it's in the Bible when in fact it's not. You can be sure that the Bible is full of information about salvation, and it is very clear that we are saved only by God's grace through Jesus Christ. Now, to be clear, no Bible verse says, "You must accept Jesus Christ as your Savior before you die," and that's not what you're asking. What you want is evidence that this is what the Bible teaches. So what we're going to do is take you through a few verses that point to this. You can look up these verses on your own.

First we have to find what the Bible says about the human condition. Here you need to read Romans 3:23, which says that every person has sinned and falls short of God's perfect standard. Next you have to consider the death penalty for sin (for that go to Romans 6:23). The conclusion of Scripture is unmistakable: Every person is a sinner, and sin leads to death. Not good for the human race!

Now go to John 3:16, the most popular verse in the Bible. This verse clearly explains that God sent Jesus into the world so that all who believe in Him would have eternal life. Everyone still dies in the physical sense, but those who put their faith in Jesus will have eternal life.

Finally, we need to know that the only way to have eternal life is through Jesus Christ. He is the only way we can be saved from eternal death (John 14:6; Acts 4:12). And the only way to receive salvation through Jesus is through faith. Our good deeds won't do it (Ephesians 2:8-9).

We could show you many other verses, but these are some of the clearest. Hope this helps answer your question. May God bless you!

Why did Jesus come when He did?

I just finished *Knowing God 101,* and I loved it. The book was informative and easy to read. I have been a Christian for many years, but this gave me some new perspectives. I do have a question. I hate to even mention it because I feel pretty stupid. I know that Jesus is God's Son and was sent to earth to die for us. I understand all of that. My question is, why was He sent at the time He was? Was the world that corrupt? And on the same note, weren't people sacrificing animals for their sins? Were their sins so huge that the animals just didn't cover them anymore? Or were the people trusting in rituals and not giving God their hearts—is that why Jesus was needed at the time? It sounds ridiculous I know, but what would have happened if Jesus had never come? Would we all go to hell or still be sacrificing animals?

As they used to say in school, no question is a dumb question. In fact, your questions are excellent. They indicate that you are doing some deep thinking about your faith. That's great!

You asked about the reason for the timing of Christ's coming to earth. First, we need to understand why Christ had to come. A great passage to read in this regard is Romans 5:12-21. When sin entered the world soon after God created humanity, we were in need of a Savior. God made it clear that disobedience would mean death, and that's what we got: the death penalty (Romans 6:23). Jesus didn't come at the time He did because people were more corrupt than ever before. He came because sin has corrupted the entire human race.

We don't know why Jesus came when He did, but we know this was the time set by God. Galatians 4:4 says this:

"But when the right time came, God sent his Son, born of a woman, subject to the law."

The practice of sacrificing animals was part of the old covenant. That's the system God put into place in order to show His people that keeping God's perfect standards is impossible. The fact is that every person falls short (Romans 3:23). Animal sacrifice was also a precursor to the perfect blood sacrifice that Jesus made on the cross (read Hebrews 9:11-15). The key is that only Jesus was able to live a sinless life, and only He is the perfect sacrifice. "That is why he is the one who mediates the new covenant between God and people, so that all who are invited can receive the eternal inheritance God has promised them" (Hebrews 9:15).

If Jesus had never come, we would have no opportunity to receive God's eternal inheritance. But that was never an option for God. God's holiness demands punishment for sin, and His love motivates Him to save us from our sins.

Are the Father, Son, and Holy Spirit equal?

We are told that the Father, the Son, and the Holy Spirit are all equal. I guess I don't quite understand. If they are equal, how does the Father send the Son to save us from our sins by dying on the cross and overcoming death three days later? I assume that I am thinking in human terms, as if my earthly father would send me on a mission.

You're right about trying to think about this incredibly complex subject from an earthly standpoint. It isn't easy! But it's worthwhile. God wants us to think our thoughts after Him. In the doctrine of salvation, all three Persons in the Trinity—God the Father, Jesus the Son, and the Holy Spirit—participate. To get a mental picture, see the Father saving you with two hands. One hand is the Son, who *accomplished* your salvation by His work on the cross. The other hand is the Holy Spirit, who *applies* your salvation by His work in your life as you live each day. Another way to look at it is that Jesus *saves* you, and the Holy Spirit *seals* you (read Ephesians 1:9-14).

In terms of sending His Son, God did this so that Jesus could pay the legal debt of sin on your behalf (it's called *justification*), and He sent the Holy Spirit to guarantee your salvation.

? How can Jesus be the Messiah?

I have a question about the Trinity. If Jesus was fathered by God or the Holy Spirit, how can He be the Messiah? The Old Testament prophecies say Messiah has to be from the lineage of King David. Matthew 1 says Messiah is from the line of Solomon. Luke 3 says from the line of Nathan. Which is correct? If the New Testament writers could not even agree on the grandparents, how can we believe the other parts?

Jesus was not fathered by God or the Holy Spirit. God the Father, God the Son, and God the Holy Spirit have existed eternally as three Persons in one God. Jesus is God incarnate (in the flesh). He is the Messiah foretold by the Old Testament prophets, and He fulfilled everything the prophets said about the Messiah.

To understand the genealogies of Jesus, you have to consider their contexts. The genealogy of Matthew is the genealogy of Joseph. It includes 41 names in descending order going back to Abraham. It includes David's line through Solomon. This is the messianic line, and it is a legal link, not a physical one. The genealogy of Luke is the genealogy of Mary. It includes 74 names in ascending order and goes back to Adam. It includes David's line through Nathan. This traces the human roots of Jesus. Both genealogies are correct.

Does Genesis 1:26 prove the Trinity?

I've got a follow-up question about the Trinity. You use Genesis 1:26 as proof that God is in three Persons. How can this be? If you read the Hebrew and check the grammar, you will see that a singular pronoun is used.

The verse reads, "Then God said, 'Let us make people in our image, to be like ourselves.'" A case cannot be made for a singular pronoun. What some commentators do is interpret the plural as a "plural of majesty," indicating dignity and greatness. However, the plural form of *Elohim,* the word for God, can be explained in the same way. The correct interpretation—the one overwhelmingly favored by orthodox tradition going back to the third century—is that the narrative here in Genesis presents God as calling on the other two members of the Trinity in the creation event.

Was Jesus fully God?

I have been a believer for 32 years, and after studying your book on John, I have a question that never occurred to me before. If Jesus was fully God when He was on earth, was He omniscient, omnipresent, and omnipotent? Matthew 24:36 seems to indicate He wasn't omniscient, and John 5:30 seems to indicate He wasn't omnipotent. And what indication is there that He was omnipresent? In other words, how was Jesus fully God? Thank you for the opportunity to submit questions. I truly appreciate the simplicity and clarity of your writing, as well as your availability to your readers.

You've touched upon one of the truly great and difficult controversies of the church—and it began in the third century. Basically, you are asking about the doctrine of *christology,* which involves the Person of Christ. The controversy is about His divine and human natures and how they relate to each other. We're going to give you the two historical views, both of which are orthodox (that is, correct).

Alexandrian Christology teaches that the Person of Christ is the *Logos,* who assumed a human nature. There is a flow of divine attributes (such as omniscience and omnipotence) to the human nature of Christ. Without the divine flow, there is no complete, freestanding man. This is known as Word-flesh Christology (as in "the word became flesh"—see John 1:14). This view is sometimes referred to as the "hypostatic union." The shortcoming of this view is that it has a tendency to ignore Christ's real humanity.

Antiochene Christology emphasizes the integrity of the two natures. Jesus' humanity stays human and His divine nature stays divine. There is no flow of attributes. The main motive for this view is that the deity of Christ is separated from the man who suffered. This is known as Word-man Christology, and the union is described as "sympathetic." The key verse is Colossians 2:9. The shortcoming of this view is that you end up with a split personality.

The verses you reference indicating that Jesus didn't have the divine attributes are used by those who fall more into the Antiochene camp. The Alexandrian view would hold that all of the attributes were imparted to the human Jesus.

This controversy over the two natures of Christ continued until 451, when the Council of Chalcedon met and arrived at a compromise of sorts. This council didn't really solve the problem, but it did set boundaries, including these:

- Christ is true God and true man.

- He has the same nature as the Father with regard to His Godhood.

- He has the same nature as man with regard to His manhood.

- He is like us except without sin.

- The two natures of Christ exist without confusion or division.

- The distinctives of each nature are retained.

The bottom line is that this topic is one of the true and great mysteries of Scripture (like the Trinity). We know that Jesus was fully God and fully man, but we don't know how this works. If Jesus had every attribute of God all the time, then how could He identify with us? But if He didn't have the Father's attributes, then how could He effectively die for our sins? We also know from Philippians 2:6-7 that Jesus did not "demand and cling to his rights as God." Instead, He voluntarily "took on the humble position of a slave and appeared in human form." This is how He was able to die for our sins.

You can take comfort in the fact that some of the greatest minds and most deeply spiritual people in the history of the church have wrestled with this issue for centuries—and still we don't know completely how it works. The fact that you are wrestling with this shows that you are moving on in your spiritual life. You are going deep. Keep studying and keep praying. And may God bless your serious inquiry!

Was Jesus both God and man?

I am a fairly new Christian. I have read the New Testament and can't find a passage that says Jesus was God and man at the same time. I don't see any verses in any of the Gospels where Jesus referred to Himself as God after the Word became flesh and before His resurrection. I have seen a lot of places where He referred to Himself as the Son of God, the Son of Man, a prophet, and a teacher, but not as God and man. Maybe you can straighten me out on this matter. I love Him just the same either way, I know that I am born again (because of Romans 10:9-10), and I am still teachable.

First of all, we appreciate your tender heart and teachable spirit. You are going to go far in your Christian life with that attitude! You said you haven't found any verses where Jesus referred to Himself as God. Believe it or not, the disciples had this same question! In John 14:8, Philip said, "Lord, show us the Father and we will be satisfied." Jesus replied, "Philip, don't you even yet know who I am, even after all the time I have been with you? Anyone who has seen me has seen the Father! So why are you asking to see him? Don't you believe that I am in the Father and the Father is in me?" (John 14:9-10). Clearly Jesus was saying that He and the Father were one. They are not the same Person, but they are of the same substance.

What color was Jesus' skin?
Does anything in spiritual teachings reflect the color of Jesus' skin?

The Bible doesn't specifically tell us the color of Jesus' skin, but Jesus was a Jew, born of the seed of Abraham, the father of the Jewish nation (Genesis 12:1-3). You can read about the ancestry of Jesus in Matthew 1:1-17. Because of Jesus' ethnic origin, we can assume that He looked like a Jew, with dark hair, dark eyes, and an olive complexion.

Did Jesus have a son?

I'm very fascinated with Christian apologetics, and I wish to learn as much as I can in order to answer "stumbling" questions people ask. Just yesterday a friend told me she had watched a documentary on television about some aspects of Jesus' life. The documentary made outrageous statements, such as Jesus having a son and that Mary Magdalene was His girlfriend. I tried explaining to my friend that a lot of legendary literature is out there and that she should be looking for reliable evidence that backs up such twisted claims, but she kept telling me she saw on the show that they had "proof," though she was unable to quote the source of these claims. So my question is this: Where do these claims originate? Have you heard them before? If so, please let me know so I can explain it to my friend.

Thanks for your e-mail. We commend you for the way you responded to your friend. We are aware of the television special she saw, and you are right. It's about legendary literature that no reputable New Testament scholar—we repeat, no reputable scholar—accepts as true.

What is fueling all of this is the phenomenal bestselling book *The DaVinci Code* by Dan Brown. We've read the book, and we can tell you that it is pure fiction. Yet many people read it or hear about the legends and quote it as truth. There is no proof. Your friend would not be able to find any proof even if she tried because it isn't there.

You are correct that honest seekers should be looking for the truth about the Bible and the life of Christ. It's out there and easily accessible. On the life of Christ, we recommend *The Case for Christ* by Lee Strobel. To answer specific questions raised by *The DaVinci Code,* we recommend *Breaking the DaVinci Code* by Darrell Bock, a New Testament scholar.

We commend you for wanting to learn as much as you can so you can answer those "stumbling" questions people have. You are doing exactly what the Bible says you should do: "And if you are asked about your Christian hope, always be ready to explain it. But you must do this in a gentle and respectful way" (1 Peter 3:15-16). Don't feel threatened by the kind of questions your friend is asking. Instead, see them as an opportunity to explain your faith. You will be amazed at how God will use your words to strengthen you even as He uses them to reach people without hope.

Did Jesus really die on the cross?

I have a big concern about my sister. She does not know anything about my faith and questions a lot of what I believe. I'm worried because she is studying with Jehovah's Witnesses. I have begun to answer some of her questions, but I don't know how to prove to her that Jesus died on a cross. I showed her passages in the New Testament, but she doesn't believe the Bible I read. She showed me a Bible that stated that Jesus died on a stake. And when we think of a stake, we think of a straight pole or a stick. She says that's why Jehovah's Witnesses don't believe Jesus died on a cross. The only thing I can tell her is that crucifixion was a method the Romans used to put people to death, and didn't they use a cross for that? Please help me to explain this better or find a source where I can show her proof.

I'm not a devout Christian yet, but I have been praying to God to fill my heart with the Holy Spirit so that I may follow Him and help others to follow Him as well. Also, your book *Knowing the Bible 101* has answered many of my questions about the Good Book. I am currently reading it again, and I find that I'm learning more. Little by little my family is growing strong in their faith, which is wonderful, but I'm concerned about my sister. Thanks for your help!

Thanks for your e-mail. We're not surprised that your sister has doubts about the crucifixion. With all the interest created by *The Passion of the Christ,* many people—including the Jehovah's Witnesses—are disputing the historical facts of the Bible. There's no question that there was a crucifixion and that it took place the way the Bible describes. In fact, you won't find any credible scholars who dispute the historical fact of the crucifixion. Why is this? First, you have the Bible itself, widely considered the most reliable historical document of the ancient world. Besides the Bible, numerous Roman and Jewish historians verify the fact of the crucifixion. The most famous historian is Josephus, who lived from AD 37 to 100. Here's what he wrote in his book *Antiquities:*

> Now there was about this time Jesus, a wise man, if it be lawful to call him a man, for he was a doer of wonderful works, a teacher of such men as receive the truth with pleasure. He drew over to him both many of the Jews, and many of the Gentiles. He was the Christ, and when Pilate, at the suggestion of the principal men among us, had condemned him to the cross, those that loved him at the first did not forsake him, for he appeared to them alive again the third day; as the divine prophets had foretold these and ten thousand other wonderful things concerning him. And the tribe of Christians so named from him are not extinct at this day.

The problem with Jehovah's Witnesses is that their main goal is to discredit Jesus as the Son of God, equal to God in every way. So it's not surprising that your sister has been given false information. Pray for her (as we know you are) and love her. And when you can, share the truth with her. That's all you can do. The rest is up to her.

As for you, continue to sincerely seek God. He promises to reward you if you do (Hebrews 11:6).

Chapter 3
The Holy Spirit

When considering the Trinity, many people seem to have an understanding of God (our heavenly Father) and Jesus (who walked on the earth). But we have received many questions about the Holy Spirit. This third Person of the Trinity seems to be more mysterious. How does He work in our lives? Do we receive supernatural powers from Him? How does all of this happen?

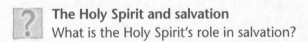

The Holy Spirit and salvation
What is the Holy Spirit's role in salvation?

Here is a theological understanding of the Holy Spirit's role in salvation. Jesus operates vicariously in salvation. In other words, He was our substitute (our vicar) before God, who saves us by His grace when we accept the Person and work of Jesus by faith (Ephesians 2:8-9). The Spirit of God actually indwells us, and He baptizes us into the body of Christ the moment we receive Him (1 Corinthians 12:13).

Because the Spirit indwells us, Christ lives in us. Christologically, Christ is seated at the right hand of God the Father.

Pneumatologically, the Holy Spirit has been poured out on all flesh, indwelling those who belong to Christ.

A good passage to read in this regard is Ephesians 3:14-19.

? What is "speaking in tongues"?

Hello! I love your television show, *Christianity 101*. It has wonderfully helped me understand more about God and His Word. I've really been amazed by the power of the Holy Spirit, and one of my questions is how people can speak in tongues. I know it is the language of the Spirit, but is it a gift to certain people? Or can anybody who has the Holy Spirit in their hearts speak in tongues? I love God, and I am trying my best to live for Him and to learn more about Him.

You asked about the Holy Spirit and the gift of tongues. First of all, understand that tongues is a spiritual gift. Every Christian has at least one spiritual gift (the gifts are listed in Romans 12:6-8; 1 Corinthians 12:4-11,23-31; and Ephesians 4:11-12).

God gives spiritual gifts to empower us to serve Him and to serve others (1 Corinthians 12:7; 1 Peter 4:10). They are not for our self-edification.

The gift of tongues appeared in the book of Acts for a specific purpose—so the believers could proclaim the good news about Christ to people in their own language. Should tongues always be in known languages, or at least able to be interpreted? Bible scholars disagree. Some believe that tongues should be, while others see evidence that the gift of tongues can also be a type of private worship language. Church historians point to times of great spiritual renewal, during which the gift of tongues seems to be more evident. We seem to be in such a time!

To keep the gift of tongues in balance, read 1 Corinthians 14. A key verse is 1 Corinthians 14:19. And in 1 Corinthians 12:31, Paul advises us to desire "the most helpful gifts."

Is it necessary to receive the Holy Spirit?

I went to church a couple of nights ago, and the preacher talked about the Holy Ghost baptism. The message was basically telling us that all Christians don't receive the Holy Ghost baptism and that speaking in tongues is a sign that you are filled with the Holy Ghost. Is that true? Also, at the end of the service, he asked us to come to the altar and pray for the Holy Ghost and was trying to get me to speak in tongues. Is this the way it should be done? I asked him a question at the end of the service based on a comment that he made. He said, "The Holy Ghost seals your salvation." Can somebody go to heaven without the baptism of the Holy Ghost? Is it necessary that I receive the Holy Ghost?

Let's see if we can help sort this out.

The Bible is very clear that all Christians receive the Holy Spirit. In fact, the Holy Spirit is the one who makes your salvation possible. Jesus said, "The truth is, no one can enter the Kingdom of God without being born of water and the spirit. Humans can reproduce only human life, but the Holy Spirit gives new life from heaven" (John 3:5-6).

The Holy Spirit baptizes every believer into the body of Christ (1 Corinthians 12:13). You cannot be a believer without the baptism of the Holy Spirit. The pastor is right that the Holy Spirit seals your salvation. But He does this for every believer! He is the guarantee that Jesus is coming back for us someday.

Now, what your church may be talking about is a "second blessing" of the Holy Spirit. This is something many charismatic churches emphasize. Your church may very well refer to this as "Holy Ghost baptism." It seems to be a fuller expression of the Holy Spirit, and we see this as compatible with Scripture. However, any time a church teaches that this second blessing must be accompanied by speaking in tongues, we would take exception.

Speaking in tongues is a spiritual gift that not every believer possesses. There are many spiritual gifts—see 1 Corinthians 12:8-11 for a partial list—and tongues is one of the gifts. However, you need to read the context. Read all of 1 Corinthians 12, and you will see that the Holy Spirit distributes these gifts, and we all have different gifts. That's the way God designed the body of Christ to function.

What is true baptism of the Holy Spirit?

In your book *Knowing the Bible 101,* you say that Spirit baptism is the way God brings you into the body of Christ or the church, and that you don't have to ask for it. If this is the case, then how do you explain that Jesus instructed the apostles "to wait for the gift my Father promised" in Acts 1:5, and when the gift arrived in Acts 2:2-4, they were filled with the Holy Spirit, with the evidence of speaking in tongues? I personally, along with many other believers, see the baptism of the Holy Spirit as a separate experience and much to be desired...an added tool. What is your insight on this?

The reason the apostles had to wait was that the Holy Spirit had not yet come. Once the Holy Spirit came (in Acts 2), He stayed for good. We don't have to ask the Holy Spirit to come to us because the Holy Spirit is the one who baptizes us into the body of Christ (1 Corinthians 12:13).

With regard to the Holy Spirit, we are never commanded to be baptized in or with the Holy Spirit because that is how we are saved. What we are commanded to do is to be *filled* with the Holy Spirit (Ephesians 5:18). Study that verse. We are commanded to not get drunk with wine, but to be controlled (or filled) with the Holy Spirit. Giving our lives to the Holy Spirit's control every moment is a willful act on our part.

As for speaking in tongues, yes, the Holy Spirit's coming to the apostles was accompanied by speaking in tongues. However, if you read the passage carefully, you will see that the tongues were in the known languages of the people gathered in Jerusalem. Each one could hear the gospel message in his or her own language. The Holy Spirit came as a powerful sign that Jesus was among them, and it served to bring 3000 people into God's kingdom on that day.

Now, speaking in tongues can be a prayer language. Paul talks about that. We know many people who speak in tongues as a prayer language, but none of them believe that speaking in tongues is a requirement for salvation. In fact, in 1 Corinthians 14 Paul speaks of tongues as a lesser gift.

Don't make speaking in tongues the central issue of your faith. You are saved by faith alone in Christ alone by God's grace alone (Ephesians 2:8-9). You can add nothing to your salvation. When you receive Christ, you are baptized into the body of Christ by the Holy Spirit.

Speaking in tongues and receiving a "second blessing" of the Holy Spirit is entirely appropriate, and it can be a wonderful thing. But don't be teaching people that they have to seek for the Holy Spirit's baptism in order to be saved. That will foster confusion. The Holy Spirit is not the author of confusion, as you know.

Please hear us. We are completely in favor of speaking in tongues, but it's not for everyone. It's a spiritual gift, not a spiritual fruit. Everyone should demonstrate the fruit of the Spirit (Galatians 6), but not everyone has the same gifts.

The anointing of the Holy Spirit

What makes some people desire the anointing more than others?

We assume you mean the anointing of the Holy Spirit. In Scripture, anointing is a symbol for the coming of the Holy Spirit to the believer. You need to know that all believers have the Holy Spirit in their lives. The Holy Spirit is the one who makes it possible for you to be saved, because the Holy Spirit baptizes you into the body of Christ (1 Corinthians 12:13).

If you look up 1 John 2:20,27, you will see that the Holy Spirit has already come upon you. You have already received Him.

Now, the Holy Spirit can work more strongly through you as you let Him control you (Ephesians 5:18). We believe that some believers desire the Holy Spirit to control them more than others, and in this way they experience more of what He has to offer.

Indwelling and filling of the Holy Spirit

I've been struggling with this question: When does the indwelling of the Holy Spirit happen? Is it when I was born again or when the baptism of the Holy Spirit occurs? What is the difference between the indwelling and the filling of the Holy Spirit? I've read that when you are born again, the Holy Spirit enters. Is this the indwelling, or does the Holy Spirit just come into my life to guide me? The reason that I am confused is that at the church I attend they say that the Holy Spirit cannot be in me because I smoke. But I've never read any conditions that when someone accepts Jesus (and I realize that God searches my heart to determine that I'm not just giving him lip service), the Holy Spirit takes up residence. I've never read that total deliverance must take place first.

I am being really convicted by the Holy Spirit to stop smoking. I feel the Holy Spirit moving in my life and prompting me in various areas. So does the Holy Spirit now reside in me, or is it working outside of me? I've also felt the Spirit of God telling me things, but I'm hesitant to share this because I feel the pastor doesn't think I can hear from God because I smoke. *Help!*

You understand correctly that the Holy Spirit indwells you when you are born again. In fact, the Holy Spirit is the One who makes your new life in Christ possible. Jesus said, "Humans can reproduce only human life, but the Holy Spirit gives new life from heaven" (John 3:6).

The apostle Paul confirms this when he writes, "But we have all been baptized into Christ's body by one Spirit, and we have all received the same Spirit" (1 Corinthians 12:13).

You're also right that no condition would prevent the Holy Spirit from coming into your life. You're also right that total deliverance doesn't always occur when you accept Jesus Christ as your personal Savior and the Holy Spirit comes into your life. Yes, some people experience immediate release from addictions or other physical challenges, but we would say that is the exception. For most people, life in Christ is a process of growing closer to Him day by day. Think of a sick person getting well or a broken bone mending. Change takes time.

The fact that the Holy Spirit is prompting your heart is fantastic! That's what you want. It means you are allowing the Holy Spirit to fill you as well as indwell you.

Being filled by the Holy Spirit is different from indwelling. Being indwelled is automatic, but being filled is a condition of our willingness to let Him control our lives (see Ephesians 5:18). Being filled with the Holy Spirit means giving your life over to Him. It means that you don't let unconfessed sin dwell in your life (read 1 John 1:9-10). When we confess our sins, God is faithful to forgive us. You have been forgiven of your sins "positionally" because Christ died and paid the penalty for your sin, but your day-to-day life will still have sin. Deal with sin as it comes.

As you grow in your Christian life, your desire to sin will decrease. It's a function of maturity.

Now, let's talk about your smoking for a moment. First of all, don't let anyone tell you that the Holy Spirit can't dwell in you because you smoke. That's ridiculous and totally untrue! The Bible doesn't single out smoking as a sin. Scripture does talk about glorifying God in your body: "Don't you know that your body is the temple of the Holy Spirit, who lives in you and was given to you by God?...So you must honor God with your body" (1 Corinthians 6:19-20).

Yes, this applies to smoking because smoking is destructive to your body. You know that. But so is overeating. An obese Christian is abusing his or her body as much as a chain-smoking Christian. The good news is that people can lose weight, and they can kick the smoking habit. You sound determined to do that. Definitely pray and ask God to help you, but you need to get some professional help (your doctor could help you) or join a support group. Smoking is a very difficult habit to break, but you can do it with God's help.

Your smoking has nothing to do with whether or not you can hear God. The Holy Spirit is living in you, and He is convicting you. That's a sure sign He is working.

Still, some sins can prevent the Holy Spirit from filling you and working through you. If you want to read just one list, look up Galatians 5:19-21. Every Christian needs to avoid these as we avoid being controlled by our sinful nature. By contrast, when the Holy Spirit controls us, He produces spiritual fruit (see Galatians 5:22-23).

We hope this has been helpful. You are a wonderful child of God who has the Holy Spirit living in you. He will help you grow as you develop new spiritual habits that will replace your old sinful ones.

The Holy Spirit in the Old Testament
Did the Holy Spirit actually speak directly to the people in the Old Testament, or was it God? And how could they determine the difference between the two? I understand that God and the Holy Spirit are one, but what was the Holy Spirit's role in the Old Testament?

Now that's a good question! We know that all three members of the Trinity—God the Father, God the Holy Spirit, and God the Son—have always existed, and they will always exist. The one true God in three Persons is infinite and eternal.

So we know the Holy Spirit was present in the Old Testament. You're wondering what role He played and whether people could distinguish between God the Holy Spirit and God the Father.

Theologian Wayne Grudem writes in his book *Systematic Theology* that the Holy Spirit had less powerful and less extensive work in the Old Testament, but He was there (see Numbers 11:16-17; Judges 13:24-25). Moses longed for the time when the Holy Spirit would be poured out on all people (Numbers 11:29). Other Old Testament prophets looked forward to a time when the work of the Holy Spirit would be much more powerful and widespread (see Jeremiah 31:31-33; Ezekiel 36:26-27; Joel 2:28-29).

In the New Testament, the Holy Spirit came to Jesus in full power (Luke 3:21-22; 4:14). And then after Jesus ascended into heaven, the Holy Spirit came upon all believers on the Day of Pentecost (Acts 1:8).

We don't always understand God's ways, but we know they are for the best. We can thank Him that we have the full benefit of the Holy Spirit today!

? Do miracles happen today?

Do miracles happen today? I did not think so, or at least not the type we read about in the book of Acts. Why did the early church have miracles and we don't? Was it because we now have the written Bible? Please let me know.

The question as to whether or not God performs miracles today is easily answered when you consider the ways in which He works in the world. We still see healings today—and we're not talking about so-called faith healers but real healings of people who once had cancer or heart disease or a brain tumor. And some everyday events can't be explained by coincidence or chance. God is working in this world to preserve and protect His own.

As for the miracles in the book of Acts, they were spectacular—speaking in known languages, healings, and even a dead person coming back to life. Again, these things can and do happen today, but perhaps not as visibly or in such a concentrated fashion as in the early church. These miracles occurred with greater frequency to help authenticate apostolic authority. And they served to help launch the beginning of the church in dramatic fashion.

Yes, the fact that we have the complete Scriptures today is important, but Christians in the first century had most of the Scriptures as well.

Chapter 4

The Bible

The Bible is the most popular book in the world, which may explain why so many people have questions about it. Like our readers, you may be wondering how we can know that the Bible is true. What about so-called inconsistencies in the Bible? And how does a book written 2000 years ago have any relevance to your life today? Find out the answers to these questions and others in this chapter.

Can you prove the Bible is God's Word?
I believe that the Bible is God's true Word, that by divine guidance the Holy Spirit inspired its writers. How can I explain this better to someone who doesn't accept my viewpoint?

It gets down to the question of how God, who is a Spirit, wrote His Word. The way He did it is the way you explained: God inspired (breathed into) various men through the Holy Spirit to write down His message for us (2 Peter 1:20-21). A way to explain it to someone who's having difficulty is to focus on the results.

First, you have this remarkable book written by 40 different authors over a period of 1600 years. By all human measurement, this book should be filled with inconsistencies, both in message and substance. But it's totally consistent. These authors wrote as if they were in the same room together and decided to write a single book with a single theme and a consistent message. But they didn't do that. Each author wrote his book individually. Yet the theme of Jesus Christ and the redemption of humankind by a loving God are evident throughout the Bible.

Second, every detail of history is completely accurate. The Bible is the only holy book that roots itself in history so thoroughly and without error. Not every person and event in the Bible has been verified from outside sources, but a huge number have, and none has been shown to be false.

Third, the Bible contains more than 2500 prophecies. Of these, 2000 have already been fulfilled to the letter. The chances that any one book would be correct even 10 percent of the time is nearly impossible. That a book would be correct 100 percent of the time concerning 2000 prophecies is in the realm of impossibility, at least from a human perspective.

The only explanation for the Bible's consistent message, historical accuracy, and perfect prophetic record is a divine, transcendent source. No other possibilities exist. Of course, belief in the Bible as God's Word goes to the heart of a belief in God as the Creator and Sustainer of the universe. You can't have one without the other. If God is who the Bible says He is, then God could have easily given us a personal message the way He did. If God is not who the Bible says He is, then the Bible is just another book, and we are without hope in a world without purpose.

Is the New Testament true?

How do we know if the New Testament is true or cleverly written to make Jesus out to be the Messiah?

This is a very legitimate question. Someone might think that the New Testament writers studied the hundreds of Old Testament prophecies concerning the Messiah and then simply wrote down that Jesus fulfilled them all. The problem with this view is that all four of the Gospel writers—along with Paul, Peter, James, Jude, and the writer of Hebrews—would have had to conspire to make this happen, not to mention the hundreds of witnesses who saw Jesus after He was resurrected.

And even if they had conspired and agreed to make Jesus out to be the Messiah, how could they have manipulated the historical facts of the birth and life of Jesus, the many events surrounding His passion, and His crucifixion and resurrection? More than just a few people were involved in the life of Christ. The Roman government with its emperors and governors, the Jewish authorities, and thousands of ordinary people encountered Jesus in one way or another. And yet Jesus the Messiah fulfilled the prophecies written about Him hundreds of years earlier. That's not just clever. It's utterly astounding!

How do you study the Bible?

I am trying to study the Bible, and I don't know where to get started or how to study. Can you tell me what to do and where to start?

Studying the Bible can be a daunting task. The best way is to just start reading it. God will help you understand—after all, it's His Word—through the Holy Spirit (see 1 Corinthians 2:10). Now, you can do some things to help yourself out. First, make sure you have a readable translation of the Bible. The King James Version has its place, but it's a little tough for most of us to understand today. If you don't have a modern translation of the Bible, we recommend that you buy one. Our personal favorite is the New Living Translation. Another good one that a lot of churches use is the New International Version. If you can afford it, purchase a *Life Application Study Bible* in either translation.

As for actually reading the Bible, being systematic is better than hunting and pecking your way through. We suggest starting in a couple of areas. First, to get a good overview of the life of Christ, read the Gospel of Mark. Read one chapter a day or even less. The key is to be consistent. At the same time, read a Psalm each day. You will get a feel of the Psalm writers' passion for God.

We also recommend that you get a book about the Bible, one that will help you understand how the Bible is put together, how each of the 66 books in the Bible relates to the Bible as a whole, and how you can study the Bible most effectively. We have two recommendations. One is our own *Knowing the Bible 101* (how's that for a shameless plug?), and another excellent resource is *How to Study the Bible for All Its Worth* by Gordon Fee and Douglas Stuart.

Finally, if you aren't doing this already, find and attend a church where the pastor teaches from the Bible. This will help you immensely as you try to make sense of God's Word and grow in your Christian life.

What's the best Bible translation?

Hello from Singapore! I really have to thank God that I found your book *Knowing the Bible 101* while browsing in a Christian bookshop. Before that I was really troubled over the fact that I was studying the wrong Bible—the New International Version. My friend believes wholeheartedly in the King James Version. She says that is the one and only Bible that Christians should read. According to her, the other versions are not God's words. We had a debate over this, and I was a little affected by it. When I dedicated my life to God, I was already reading the NIV and was very comfortable with it. Now I'm not so sure. What is your view on this?

Preferring a particular Bible translation over any others is natural. But to say that one Bible translation is the only one Christians should read is not helpful. Keep in mind that the original Bible manuscripts were written in Hebrew (Old Testament) and Greek (New Testament), so if any version were closest to "God's words," the original version would be. In fact, Bible scholars will tell you that only the original manuscripts are inspired. Unfortunately, the original manuscripts don't exist anymore, but we do have very reliable copies, and from those copies all the different Bible translations have been made. We believe that God, through the Holy Spirit, also guides Bible translators. After all, God is always about getting His Word into as many hands as possible, so why wouldn't He be interested in guiding the people who translate His Word into other languages? Bible translation—whether into English or any of the other languages the Bible has been translated into—is a high calling. We can be thankful for the scholars who have given their lives—sometimes literally—in order to bring the Bible into a more understandable language.

The King James Version, first published in 1611, was an excellent translation of the Bible into English, and it remains very popular to this day. But it is only one version of the Bible, no better than many other excellent versions done since then. In fact, the King James Version has gone through a dozen revisions since 1611, so when people say you should only be reading the King James Version, you could ask them which version they mean!

The key to finding and reading a good Bible translation is to choose one that you can understand. If the King James Version is the easiest to understand, then read it. But if the New International Version is the clearest, then read that one. As long as the version you are reading is a faithful and accurate translation of the original languages and retains the Bible's original intent, it's perfectly fine. Besides that, we are never to worship the Word of God, only the God of the Word.

The first Bible

When was the first Bible published?

The first Bible to be published, as in printed, was the Gutenberg Bible in 1455. Gutenberg developed the first commercially successful printing press, and the first book he printed was the Bible (it was in Latin). Prior to that time, every Bible (and every book, for that matter) had to be copied by hand. Now, there were Bibles before Gutenberg. John Wycliffe produced the first English Bible in 1384. He translated it from the Latin Vulgate, which was first translated from the original Hebrew and Greek in 405 by Jerome.

The Dead Sea Scrolls

My daughter, who was born again two years ago, asked me this morning, "If the Dead Sea Scrolls were just located in the twentieth century, how did the Bible get written before then?"

Actually, the Dead Sea Scrolls, which were discovered in a cave at Qumran in 1949, are not the only Bible manuscripts in existence. Scholars knew about many other scrolls long before the Dead Sea Scrolls were found. What makes the

Dead Sea Scrolls unique is that they are the oldest manuscripts yet discovered (scholars generally date them between 100 BC and AD 68). In other words, they were written closer to the actual events, which makes them even more reliable. What's interesting is that even though these older manuscripts were found, they did not change the content of the Bible, showing that the Bible and the manuscripts upon which it is based are very reliable.

? How is the Bible organized?

I would like to buy and read and study the Bible primarily by myself. I have never read the Bible before, and I know virtually nothing about it. Even though I saw your television program, *Christianity 101,* on how the Bible is organized, I don't have an adequate structure to plug into to keep it in proper order. Is it organized chronologically or what?

The Bible is generally in chronological order, but some sections don't fit into a chronology, such as the books of poetry and wisdom in the Old Testament. In the New Testament, the Gospels are somewhat chronological, but they overlap (four different voices writing about the same subject—Jesus). The book of Acts is very chronological, but then you have the letters of Paul, James, Peter, John, Jude, and the book of Hebrews. These have been placed in the Bible, not in chronological order but by category and then by size. For example, the letters of Paul are first, and they are arranged from the longest to the shortest. Then come the general epistles, and they are in the same kind of order. Even this general format has exceptions.

If chronology really interests you, check out an excellent resource called *The Narrated Bible,* which has been compiled by F. LeGard Smith. He does a wonderful job of blending Scriptural narration into one continuous story.

? Does the Bible contain inconsistencies?

I am continuing my reading of the Bible, page by page and footnote by footnote, and it seems to me there are some glaring inconsistencies. Most of them don't bother me much, and I'm trying to withhold judgments until I finish the whole Bible. But I am still troubled at how casual the chosen people were about killing. For example, in one particular episode (1 Samuel 18:24-27), David (one of God's most favored according to the Bible, and at a time when the Israelites were obeying God's will), went out with his men and killed 200 Philistines for Saul's daughter in marriage. That seems like a pretty casual regard for human life in spite of the commandments. Even my highly footnoted Bible, which offers meticulous background on unknown words and odd practices, doesn't even attempt to deal with such problem passages. I'm not trying to be argumentative, but this seems barbaric.

You have raised two issues. One, what you refer to as "glaring inconsistencies." Two, you have problems with all the killing in the Bible. Great issues!

People commonly see inconsistencies in the Bible. In fact, a thorough and honest study will show *apparent* inconsistencies that can be resolved. Remember that the Bible has been scrutinized by millions of people—including the world's brightest scholars and harshest critics—for nearly 2000 years, and no inconsistency has surfaced that cannot be reasonably resolved. We can expect this to be true because God is the author of the Scriptures and cannot lie or contradict Himself. We certainly appreciate your willingness to get through the entire Bible before you bring up specifics, but if you run across a troublesome "inconsistency," we will be happy to address it.

As to the killing, that is another matter. The bloodshed recorded in the Bible is difficult to understand. Keep in mind that the Bible records certain things that God may or may not approve of. The Bible doesn't gloss over the sinfulness and frailties of the human race, including those who follow after God, such as David. Later in David's life, you are going to read about something he did to Uriah, the husband of Bathsheba, which greatly displeased the Lord. David paid a dear price for his action, even though God forgave him.

Regarding the passage you are referencing, it was a common practice in Ancient Near East warfare to mutilate the bodies of slain enemies, as was the practice of rendering service to the father as a dowry. The other thing to keep in mind is that the Philistines were in the same category as the Canaanites. They were pagan people declared by God to be off limits. We may not understand why God allowed these things to happen, but we can understand His desire for the Israelites to be completely separated from all pagan people and practices.

? How does the Bible apply to us today?

Many passages in the Old and New Testament appear to be conversations between individuals or groups of people many, many years ago. I don't always understand how a conversation between people hundreds of years ago relates to me today. When Jesus was talking to someone, were His words not directed to that particular circumstance or person? How can I understand that all the passages or written words in the Bible apply to me today? I hope this question makes sense to you, because it doesn't sound like I'm communicating very well. I guess you can see that I'm confused.

Just because something is old doesn't mean it can't help us today. Some of the most profound wisdom about love, relationships, and basic human need was written by people like Plato, Cicero, Shakespeare, and Lincoln hundreds or even thousands of years ago. Yet we don't say, "Well, since the Declaration of Independence was written more than 225 years ago, all that stuff about human rights and freedom doesn't really apply to us today." No, we treasure those documents because they transcend time. A truth about freedom or justice is true regardless of when it was written.

This especially holds true for the Bible, the greatest book ever written. Even people who don't accept what the Bible says about God and Jesus and the condition of the human race will agree that it is the most influential book ever written. The conversations recorded between real historical characters are some of the most memorable in all of history. When you consider the fact that the Bible is about God, the Creator of the universe, and Jesus Christ, God's only Son sent into the world in real time, then the Bible becomes even more remarkable. Think of it. The Bible is God's Word to humanity. Even more, it's His personal message to you, someone He created and knows intimately and loves extravagantly.

Now, we will admit that the Bible can sometimes be overwhelming. The events happened so long ago in a different culture and a different part of the world. Yet we can learn a lot from them. The thing is, it takes effort. Yes, you can read the Bible without knowing anything about the background of a particular book or passage and get something out of it. But when you know the history, the circumstances, and the reasons behind the writing, then the Bible becomes much clearer and more enjoyable. Not only that, but you can better apply the message to your life.

You are very wise to be concerned about applying the Bible to your life. The Bible isn't just a book to read and admire. Because the Bible is the inspired Word of God, it is intended to show you how to live. Here's what the apostle Paul wrote to his young disciple Timothy:

> *All Scripture is inspired by God and is useful to teach us what is true and to make us realize what is wrong in our lives. It straightens us out and teaches us to do what is right. It is God's way of preparing us in every way, fully equipped for every good thing God wants us to do* (2 Timothy 3:16).

So whether you are reading a story about Abraham in the Old Testament or the words of Jesus in the New Testament, you can apply what you read to your life.

Can you prove the authenticity of the Bible?

I am a new Christian and new to the Bible. A friend and I were talking this week about the Bible's viewpoints on various topics. My friend, who was raised Catholic (as I was—I went to Catholic boarding schools and was an altar boy), told me that everything in the Bible is just a matter of interpretation, and he also said that the authenticity of the Bible has never been proven. "It is only on faith that people have to accept it," he said. In my heart, and by my faith, I accept that the Bible was inspired by God. I believe in the teachings of the Bible, but I just don't know how to respond to my friend.

Making statements like your friend did is easy. In fact, it's common. But such a statement is actually based on ignorance.

(It's also incredibly arrogant, if you want our honest opinion!) The first thing you should do is respond to your friend by saying, "Well, that's an interesting statement. Can you show me where a credible scholar of ancient documents has said that?" You see, it's one thing for someone to say, "The authenticity of the Bible has never been proven," or "The Bible is full of contradictions." But can they back it up? It's unlikely that your friend has any documentation for that statement whatsoever. It's a pejorative statement at best.

We could cite volumes of information from scholars of ancient documents (some of them not even Christians) who speak to the authenticity of the Bible as a reliable document. Here's just one quote from the noted scholar F.F. Bruce:

> There exists no document from the ancient world witnessed by so excellent a set of textual and historical testimonies and offering so superb an array of historical data on which an intelligent decision may be made. An honest [person] cannot dismiss a source of this kind. Skepticism regarding the historical credentials of Christianity is based on irrational bias.

We would suspect that the problem your friend has is not with the Bible as an authentic, reliable document but with what the Bible says. That's the real issue. As for you, go forward with confidence in the Bible as God's authentic, reliable, and personal message to you and all people about His plan and purposes for humankind and the world.

Is the Old Testament for Jews only?

My husband and I lead a small group Bible study in our home (we are part of a 14,000 member church, so these small groups are essential!). We are using your book *Knowing the Bible 101,* and we were confused about a particular statement you make. You say, "When reading the Old Testament, we must remember that this is the record of God's dealing with the Jews. We must keep everything we read in this context." What do you mean by that? You make it sound like the Old Testament wasn't meant for Gentiles, and I know that's not what you mean...but what do you mean?

We are delighted that you're using our book in your study. You're right—small groups are absolutely essential in big churches. God bless you for stepping out in leadership.

That statement about reading Scripture in context is extremely important. It's the first rule of hermeneutics (the process of getting meaning from the Bible). It's true that we can read any part of the Bible—Old Testament or New Testament—and get something out of it. All Scripture is profitable and useful (2 Timothy 3:16). But we need to always do our best to understand the context. Who was the book or passage written to? What were the circumstances surrounding the writing? Why did the author write it? Our primary objective should be to discover what God was trying to say through the writer to the audience receiving His message. Ultimately everyone is part of that audience, but we should always look for more immediate contexts for what God communicated in His Word.

Now, that doesn't mean that Gentiles can't read Scripture originally intended for God's chosen people. Of course we're going to get something out of it, and we can claim hundreds of promises for ourselves just as the Jews could claim them in their day. But our appreciation for the way God has worked in human history—to bring people back to Himself—can only increase if we understand the context and the original meaning of a particular passage. By the way, this goes for the New Testament as well.

You guys are very perceptive to ask a question like that. Most Bible studies don't attempt to "dig deeper" and uncover all the meaning of a text. It takes work, but the reward is huge. May God bless you as you continue to study His Word.

> ### Is everything we need in the Bible?
> Why haven't Christians accepted anything since a hundred years after the birth of Christ (the New Testament) as the inspired Word of God? Has God not spoken to anyone since then, or is everything we need to guide us already in the Bible?

What you're asking is why haven't any other books been added to the authoritative canon of Scripture since the New Testament was written. The reason is that the books in the Bible—Old Testament and New Testament—are the ones God inspired. By the time of Christ in the first century, the Old Testament canon had already been determined, and there is very little dispute over these 39 books. The 27 New Testament books are more commonly the object of criticism by those who think other books should have been included.

The way the New Testament canon was established was this. Church councils in the second and third centuries recognized which books were inspired and which books weren't by using the following criteria:

- They speak with God's authority.

- The were written by a man of God speaking to us as a prophet of God.

- They had the authentic stamp of God.

- They impact us with the power of God.

- The are accepted by the people of God.

God still speaks to people through various means (such as the Holy Spirit, other people, and circumstances), but His written Word is complete. The Bible contains all that is necessary to guide us.

How does the Bible differ from other books?
Those five criteria you list don't seem to hold up very well. Mormon and Islamic friends claim their religion fits all of those. How would you respond to their claims? They insist their writings and teachings speak with God's authority, were written by prophets, have the stamp of God, impact them with the power of God, and are accepted by them—the people of God. How would you explain that Christianity can claim these truths, but their religion cannot? What would your argument to these friends be? It seems to us that none of those five checkpoints are strong enough to convince a non-Christian that Christianity is the true religion, and that only our trust and faith in God can lead us to believe the Bible is the true authority.

You have asked some great questions, and we will do our best to answer them. What we need to do first is come at these questions about the Bible from a little different perspective. In comparing holy books (such as the Bible, the Book of Mormon, and the Qur'an) the first issue you have to deal with is the person of God. Do Christians, Mormons, and Muslims believe in and worship the same God? If you believe that they all do, then we would agree with you that no difference exists between the Bible, the Book of Mormon, and the Qur'an. Muhammad and Joseph Smith claimed to receive their visions from God, so you would have no answer for your Mormon and Islamic friends who believe their holy books were inspired by God. In fact, if Christians, Mormons, and Muslims worship the same God, then it really doesn't matter which religion you follow, let alone which Scripture you believe.

If the God of the Bible is the one true God, then the five criteria (which were developed by the early church fathers) need to be taken in the context of those books that qualified to be part of the Bible canon. In other words, these standards were never meant to be applied to any books other than those written by people who were inspired by God (see 2 Timothy 3:16). At the time the canon was completed, other books, such as the Gospel of Thomas, claimed to be inspired. But they didn't measure up to the five standards. To subject the Book of Mormon or the Qur'an to these standards doesn't work because they weren't even written at the time the early church councils met to recognize the final canon of Scripture. Also, keep in mind that the canon councils did not *declare* a book to be from God. Their job was to *recognize* the authority of God that was already there.

Which brings us back to the God of the Bible. Is He the final authority, or is the god of Islam or the god of Mormonism? That's what this question really comes down to. It isn't so much a matter of which book is right but who the real God is. And make no mistake about it: Neither the books nor the gods of Mormonism or Islam are the same as the Bible or the God of the Bible. Even if the followers of these other religions claim that they worship the same God, a study of their scriptures clearly tells you that their gods are not the same.

Chapter 5
Angels, Satan, and Demons

The popularity of movies and television shows about the spirit world reminds us that people have lots of questions about angels, Satan, and demons. Sure, demon possession provides a good plot for a movie, and a story about angels can make a feel-good television program. But we need to take the subject of angels and demons seriously; this is not just a subject of mere curiosity. These beings are all around us, all of the time. We should learn about them because they are fighting over us. Here are some of the sincere questions we received about this serious subject.

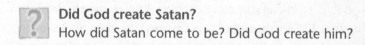

Did God create Satan?
How did Satan come to be? Did God create him?

Yes, God created Satan. Satan was an angel of the highest order. His other name, Lucifer, means "light bearer." While one of God's angels, Lucifer was "full of wisdom and perfect in beauty." But because of his beauty, he became arrogant and conceited. He considered himself to be greater than God, and he plotted to overthrow the heavenly throne. You can read more about his history in Isaiah 14:12-14.

Will angels be judged?

Okay, if God is the only eternal Spirit Being, do angels die? And if so, where do they go waiting for judgment day?

Angels are eternal spirit beings created by God. Human beings and angels are the only moral, highly intelligent creatures that God has made. There is one major difference, however. Human beings are made in God's image (Genesis 1:26-27), but the Bible never mentions that angels are. Consequently, God will someday give us authority over angels, specifically to judge them (1 Corinthians 6:3). Though we are for a little while lower than the angels (Hebrew 2:7), when our salvation is complete we will be exalted above angels and rule over them. Even now, angels serve us (Hebrew 1:14).

Already we know from Scripture that some angels sinned. They are awaiting their judgment (2 Peter 2:4). Scripture never indicates that fallen angels will have the opportunity to be saved.

Why does Satan still exist?

God will someday get rid of Satan (see Revelation 20:10). But now God is allowing Satan to exist, even though He could destroy him now. So why doesn't God get rid of Satan now?

We know that Satan is the originator of sin. He is the one who tempted Adam and Eve in the Garden of Eden. They chose to disobey God of their own free will and therefore brought sin upon the entire human race. God allowed that to happen because He wanted us to choose to obey Him freely, not as robots who could do nothing but love God. The temptation of Satan and the sin of humankind did not take God by surprise. He knew it would happen, and He always had a plan to save us through His Son, Jesus. Satan and sin continue to exist in the world because God is allowing it. Yet He also has provided a way for us to escape the death of sin and to overcome temptation. He has given us Jesus and the Holy Spirit.

These are deep doctrinal issues! There isn't an easy answer. But we must trust God that His plan is the best. Without it, we would have no hope. With Jesus we have hope and eternal life.

Someday God will deal with sin and Satan and death once and for all. Until then, we can trust that He will be faithful to us and love us with an everlasting love.

What does the Bible say about angels?

I have heard a television evangelist speak on angels on many occasions. But this one story really has me perplexed. He stated that Michael the archangel has 12 legions, and each legion contains 1000 angels. All remaining angels have only one legion each. Where is that stated in the Bible? Also, I read somewhere that in order for angels to do a particular job on earth, we must ask God to give charge to "our angel" to assist us. Can you elaborate?

We haven't heard the sermon on angels that you're talking about, so we can't comment on the teaching, but we can give you some Scripture about angels along with some commentary from a book of systematic theology by Dr. Wayne Grudem.

Scripture indicates that rank and order do exist among the angels. Most Bible versions call one angel, Michael, an archangel in Jude 9, a title that indicates rule or authority over other angels. They also call him "one of the chief princes" in Daniel 10:13. Michael also appears to be the leader in the angelic army (Revelation 12:7-8). In addition, the Lord will return from heaven with "the call of the archangel" (1 Thessalonians 4:16). Scripture does not tell about any archangels besides Michael.

Only two angels are specifically named in Scripture: Michael, as we have already said, and Gabriel (Daniel 8:16; 9:21; Luke 1:19,26).

As for how many angels God created, Scripture does not give us a number. We do know there are many! The Bible says that the chariots of God were "unnumbered thousands" (Psalm 68:17). When we worship, we are in the presence of "thousands of angels" (Hebrew 12:22). In Revelation 5:11 we read about "thousands and millions of angels."

The angels may be arranged the way the evangelist describes, but there's no evidence in Scripture to support it. He may be drawing upon military systems of organization to come up with his system.

You also wondered if angels can't do a particular job on earth unless we ask God to give charge to "our angel" to assist us. That's not exactly right. God is the one who orders His angels to protect us. We can certainly pray and ask God to protect us, but He isn't waiting for our command to send His angels to protect us. Also, there doesn't seem to be any compelling evidence in Scripture that each one of us has an individual "guardian angel" assigned to us. Rhoda's confusion of Peter and "his angel" (Acts 12:15) is probably not something we should build a doctrine on.

Do people sometimes see or hear angels?

I am a baby Christian so to speak, and I started having a thirst and hunger to know God. I started reading books and listening to gospel music, and I'm always praying when I get up in the morning and also during the day when I am working. I am a caregiver, and I take care of elderly men and women or couples in their private homes. On one occasion I was taking care of a couple who were in their early 80s. I usually include them in my prayers and thank God for their lives and the opportunity I have to take care of them. Two weeks before Christmas, the old man told me that he kept hearing a song play over and over again. So I told him maybe it was the radio or television playing the same tune, but he kept saying, "No, I hear it in my head playing." I continued to question him and ask him what kind of a song he was hearing, and he said it was a Christian song, and it is the same song playing over and over again.

Then on Christmas Day the most amazing thing happened. After our Christmas dinner and family members left, the old man was tired, and I took him to bed. About 30 minutes later, he came wheeling into the kitchen where I was, and he looked around and asked me, "Where is the choir?" I said, "What choir?" He said, "Why, the choir that is singing in here! I can hear them singing from the bedroom." I looked up and smiled and told him that the choir had left, and he looked at me with a puzzled expression and said, "I better go to bed now." Ever since then I have been wondering and trying to understand what those two events meant or illustrated to me or to the old man. Thank you for listening.

Your story about your work as a caregiver is fascinating. It's difficult to know what to make of the old man hearing a song and then a choir, but we would not be surprised if he's hearing angels! God can use angels to give us comfort in times of stress, so God could very possibly be sending His angels to give comfort for this dear man.

We also have no doubt that your prayers for him and his wife are instrumental in bringing him God's comfort. "The earnest prayer of a righteous person has great power and wonderful results" (James 5:16).

What about horoscopes?

How would you go about convincing someone that believing in so-called good luck charms (such as a rabbit's foot), pyramids, blue dots, and zodiac horoscopes only opens the door to evil spirits?

The simple answer is that none of these things are of God. So the question your friend has to ask is this—if they aren't of God, then what are they? There are only two choices: Either they are worthless, empty trinkets and systems, or they are from evil spirits.

Now, we don't think the things you listed are from evil spirits. Probably the bigger problem is that someone who puts their faith is in them going to exclude God. We don't think you can put your faith in good luck charms and horoscopes and also put your faith in God.

Did God create angels?

In Genesis the sons of God had sex with women and produced offspring. Did God create angels and have them procreate with each other? For what reason? I'm not able to get an answer from Scripture. Thank you very much for responding.

Hebrew scholar Gleason Archer writes that in the Old Testament, the term "sons of God" is used to refer either to angels or men who are true believers. He believes the evidence from the text indicates that the phrase here in Genesis 6 refers to "members of the covenant family, descendants of the line of Seth."

Therefore, what you have in Genesis 6:1-2,4 is the first occurrence of mixed marriage between believers and unbelievers, or between God's people and pagans. With this union you get the complete loss of testimony for the Lord and a total surrender of moral standards. In this passage, instead of remaining true to God and loyal to their spiritual heritage, the descendants of the godly line of Seth succumbed to the lure of the "beautiful women of the human race." The result of these unions was that the human race sank deeper and deeper into moral depravity until the wickedness of the human race broke God's heart.

Does Satan cause accidents?

My question is whether or not the devil is in charge of the weather. Does he have the power to create tornadoes, snowstorms, lightning, and floods? Does he cause car accidents?

God is in charge of the weather. In fact, He is in charge of everything in the universe. The Bible says that Christ, who is the visible image of the invisible God (Colossians 1:15), holds all creation together (Colossians 1:17). In return, the heavens declare God's glory (Psalm 19:1).

Now, this doesn't mean the universe is operating the way it's supposed to. Because of sin, creation is under God's curse (Genesis 3:17-19; Romans 8:20). All creation is waiting for the day "when it will join God's children in glorious freedom from death and decay" (Romans 8:21). Meanwhile, creation is "groaning" (Romans 8:22). We believe that's why we have natural disasters. Yet, we can be thankful that our world operates at near perfection because of God's grace and love for us.

Satan does not cause accidents either. He is an evil presence in the world, and he is capable of tempting and deceiving all people—even Christians. But sinful humanity is also responsible for much of the evil in the world.

Car accidents aren't in themselves evil, although horrible things can result. God allows them (but doesn't cause them) because He is sovereign and because He has given us the freedom of choice.

Hope this helps to answer your questions.

? Can we defeat Satan?

What gives Satan so much power? I know he can give you negative thoughts and make you do things against God's Word. So what makes him turn our will? Will someone please explain?

Satan is powerful, clever, and completely wicked. We must never forget that. He is the mighty enemy of God. But he is not the opposite of God. God and Satan are not in a great struggle. God is in control, and Satan can never win.

So if God is in control, why does He allow evil and Satan to exist? God has given all of His created beings free will, and that includes the angels. Satan was the mightiest of all the angels, and He chose to rebel against God, taking a third of all the angels in heaven with him. Satan is incredibly strong, but he is still subject to God. Satan runs free because God allows him to, even if we don't understand why. God is holy, and He will only put up with Satan for so long. Ultimately, Satan is going down to defeat, along with everyone who refuses to accept the saving work of Jesus Christ.

Meanwhile, you can stand firm against Satan. Resist him (James 4:7). Don't give him any opportunities to tempt you (Ephesians 4:27; 1 Timothy 5:14-15). Use prayer and the Bible to defend yourself against his schemes (Ephesians 6:10-18). You can't win the battle on your own, but He who is in you is greater than he who is in the world (1 John 4:4).

What about psychics?
Are there such things as good and bad psychics?

Well, the Bible is clear that all sorcery (that's another word for psychic powers) is wrong. Every time it's mentioned, it's in connection with one of two things—demons or fakery.

The same would apply today. If a psychic is someone who can tell the future, then you have to ask, where is the psychic getting his or her powers? If it's not from God (and believe us, it won't be), where is it from? Chances are most psychics are fakes, but there may be some who have demonic powers. Either way, it's not good.

Are God and Satan at war?
My question is this. If the supernatural struggle is between God and Satan, why do we humans get stuck in between all of this? Why do we have to suffer and be born and stuck in the middle of the battle between Satan and God? If God allows this, does He really care about every detail of our lives?

First of all, God and Satan are not in a battle. They are not equal, with one being supremely good and one being supremely bad. Satan is powerful, but his power has limits. God is all powerful. He is infinitely stronger than Satan, and He will defeat Satan forever.

Suffering is in the world because of sin. Satan tempted Adam and Eve, but they responded by their own free will. Because they disobeyed God, sin and death entered the world. In spite of our rebellion against God, He loved us so much that He sent His only Son, Jesus, to pay the penalty for our sin.

God does care about every detail in our lives. See Psalm 37:23. He cares about your work. He cares about you.

Why did Satan rebel?

We are having a great time in our small group going through the book of Romans using your study guide. Yesterday we were in chapter 5, and one of the members raised a question about a statement in your book on page 64. It reads as follows:

"Sin was present in the angelic world before Adam and Eve."

This launched a discussion about the timing of the angelic rebellion. According to Genesis 1:31, God had finished creating everything and said it was good, including angels we assume. So between Genesis 1:31 and Genesis 3:1, Satan must have rebelled in the heavens, but Adam and Eve would have already been created. So how was sin present in the angelic world before Adam and Eve? As I reread the statement, should it read, "before Adam and Eve sinned"? or "before Adam and Eve were created"? Can you give us some clarification on the time of the angelic rebellion?

Glad to hear you are having a lively romp through Romans!

Your group is pretty clever. You caught a little "creation and time" issue in that statement on page 64. You can look at this two ways, and it has to do with the "days" of creation.

If you hold the view that God created the existing physical universe in six literal days (a view known as young-earth creationism), then you would have to also believe that somewhere between Genesis 1:31 and Genesis 3:1, Satan and one-third of the angelic beings rebelled and came to earth, where Satan took on the form of a snake and deceived Adam and Eve.

If you hold the view that God created the existing physical universe in a much longer time (a view known as old-earth creationism), then you would believe that somewhere after Genesis 1:1, Satan and his demons rebelled. One clue in this view is Genesis 1:2: "The earth was empty, a formless mass cloaked in darkness. And the Spirit of God was hovering over its surface." It's possible that Satan rebelled after the initial creation event and was banished to earth, bringing his darkness with him. (The Hebrew word for "void," as it appears in the KJV, means "undistinguishable ruin.") God then infused the earth with light, separating the darkness.

This is all speculation of course. The truth is that we really don't know the timing of Satan's rebellion, just as we don't know for sure the timing of God's creation.

Now, as to the issue of Genesis 1:31, you're asking how God could declare all He had made "good" if Satan was already in rebellion.

Again, this goes to timing. God could have created the angelic beings prior to creating the universe. The term "in the beginning" in Genesis 1:1 doesn't mean the beginning of God, of course. He has always existed. It's possible that Genesis 1:1 could refer to the beginning of the physical universe, not the spiritual world. In this context, when God declared all that He had made was good, He would have been referring to the physical universe.

And then there's this thought. All that God makes, whether in the spiritual or physical world, is good even if what He made goes bad because of sin. That's because God has given His created beings free will. That's part of the goodness. So God could say that all He made was good, even if the angelic beings were in rebellion. Parallel to that, can God say now that His act of creating human beings was good even though we are in rebellion to Him? God doesn't see us as good (no one is good but God), but He created us in His image, so His creation of us is good. And by sending Jesus to pay the penalty for our sin, God made a way for us to be declared good (righteous) in His sight.

Isn't Romans amazing?!

Chapter 6
Creation and Evolution

Some of the most common questions we receive concern the origin of the universe. Most people believe God created the heavens and the earth, but many have questions about the age of the earth and whether or not the creation days are literal 24-hour days. Others want to know how the dinosaurs fit in or whether the Bible and science are compatible. We may not have all the answers, but we tackle some tough ones in this chapter.

Was the world created in six days?

I just finished your book *Creation and Evolution 101,* and I have a question. I am a homeschool mom, and until I started teaching my daughter, I had never really thought about whether the days of creation were six literal days or an extended period of time. I just knew that God did it, and I did not worry about how. (I grew up in a time when our faith was not challenged on every front.) I want to prepare my daughter to defend her faith and to be able to explain why she believes what she believes. I tell her as I teach her that we really do not know for sure how old things are. I am torn between the literal

six days and the old-earth view, and I am hoping you can
help me out.

You are right—we really do not know for sure how old the
universe is. However, the evidence from the natural world
seems to indicate an old universe. The question for the
Christian is whether or not an old universe is compatible
with the Bible. Old-earth creationists—those who favor the
view that God created the universe over the course of billions
of years—believe that it is. Young-earth creationists—those
who believe that God created the universe in six literal
days—don't think so.

There are good arguments from Scripture for both a
young-earth and an old-earth view, but our study has led us
to believe that the old-earth view is not only compatible
with science but with the Scriptures as well. To say it
another way, we don't think the old-earth creation view
conflicts with Scripture, mainly because the Hebrew word
"day" in Scripture (found in Genesis and elsewhere) allows
for three different meanings. It can mean a 12-hour day (as
in, "I worked a 12-hour day), it can mean a 24-hour day (as
in, "There are seven days in a week"), or it can mean a
longer period of time (as in, "In my day we didn't have
computers"). In the Bible, the same Hebrew word is used in
all three ways. In fact, one of the most famous uses of the
word "day" is in Psalm 90:4, where Moses (who also wrote the
book of Genesis) writes that to the Lord, a day is like a thousand years.

Now, having said all of that, we want to be very clear that
we believe God could have created the universe in six literal
days. He could have done it in six literal minutes. To limit
God and say that He had to do it one way or another is to
limit His power, which is not possible (He is, after all, all-
powerful). So why do we favor the old-earth creation view?

Because it is compatible with the evidence of age from God's created world. The young-earth creation view is possible philosophically and theologically, but it doesn't appear to be compatible scientifically.

Is the old-earth creation view legitimate?
If we believe the earth is billions of years old and that dinosaurs lived millions of years before Adam, how do we reconcile that with the biblical account that death did not enter the world until the fall of Adam? What about the belief that all animals were vegetarians until the fall? And what about the cavemen? I have to believe that the so-called cavemen were men who migrated from the time of Babel. Otherwise, we would have to believe that God created man before Adam. Anxiously awaiting your reply.

Thanks for your questions about creation, death, and cavemen. Let's take these one at a time. The issue of death before the fall is a little tricky. Those who hold to the young-earth view would say that there was no death before the fall. However, this position is a little tough to justify for two reasons. First, consider how much happened on the sixth day, when human beings were created:

- God created all land animals (Genesis 1:24-31).

- God formed man from dust.

- God planted a garden.

- Adam observed and named all of the animals.

- God promised Adam a helpmate.

- Adam searched for a helpmate.

- God put Adam to sleep for a time and formed Eve from one of his ribs.

That's a lot to cram into one 24-hour day! But let's assume for a moment that this did take place. You have a second issue, one that involves all the plants (created on day three) and animals now inhabiting the earth. It's a little tough to believe that nothing died. Even if you take the position that there were no carnivorous animals before the fall, the animals have eaten plants. When a plant (which is a living thing) is eaten, it dies. And what about the insects? Did the anteater go on a 24-hour fast? Did the fruit fly, with a life span of 24 hours, live until the fall? It's difficult to say how all of these things happened, of course, but it seems quite likely that death existed before the fall.

Now let's look at this death thing another way. What if the main issue was spiritual rather than physical death? Scripture is clear that God told Adam that he would die if he ate of the tree of knowledge (Genesis 2:17). Adam ate of the tree, and he didn't die *physically*, but he did die *spiritually*. In that sense, even though physical death existed before the fall, spiritual death did not.

Your other question concerned the cavemen. These creations (including Neanderthal and Cro-Magnon man) were hominids, not human beings. They were not created in God's image as Adam and Eve were (Genesis 1:26-27).

Were the creation days 24 hours long?

I have been reading your book *God Said It and Bang! It Happened.* If you believe that creation took millions of years, how do you explain how all the ecosystems were able to function when all the components took so long to come and work together? You state that the Bible has more than one definition for "day."

Thanks for your e-mail. Keep in mind that no one knows for sure if the creation days were literal 24-hour days or longer days or ages. There isn't even a consensus among evangelical Bible scholars. Fortunately our salvation does not rest on this issue. Christians can disagree on the timing of creation as long as we agree that God is the Creator.

As to your question about ecosystems, we should remember that not all plants and animals are interdependent. In other words, not every species of plant and animal is necessary to keep every other species of plant and animal alive. If Genesis tells us about six successive time periods rather than six successive 24-hour days, then God could have created those forms of plants and animals that are interdependent during the same time period. In fact, when you look at the basic order of creation, you will see that they are created in the basic order of dependence. For example, plants and animals were created before humanity, and yet not all plants and animals are dependent upon humans. Conversely, humans cannot exist without plants and animals.

Were the creation days longer than 24 hours?

You state that the Bible has more than one definition for "day." This is true, but the specific word in the Hebrew in these verses has always been translated into 24 hours—period. If that isn't obvious, the word "day" is preceded by the parameter of "there was morning and there was evening." Therefore, "day" is defined in the very same verse.

Most of the time the Hebrew word for "day" *(yom)* means 24 hours. However, as Hebrew scholars point out, the meaning in Genesis is determined by context, not majority vote. A good example is Genesis 2:4 (NASB): "This is the account of the heavens and the earth when they were created, in the day *(yom)* that the LORD God made earth and heaven." If "day" is always translated to mean a 24-hour period of time, as you say, then that means God created all of creation in one 24-hour day. Well, He certainly could have done that, but then you've got a conflict between Genesis 1 and Genesis 2.

As for the words "morning" and "evening," again you have to go to the Hebrew. The word for "morning" comes from a word that means "break forth," as in the "break of day" or "dawn." It doesn't have to be restricted to a 24-hour day. Think of the phrase, "the dawn of civilization." The same goes for "evening." The Hebrew word carries with it the meaning of "being darkened." It can describe the darkening or closing of a day, a life, or an era, as in "He was in the evening of his life." Or it can delineate something used or employed after dark, as in "evening wear."

Can science prove the Bible?

Science has never disproved the Bible, but the Bible continues to prove scientific data to sometimes be inaccurate. So why would you choose to allow scientific theory to explain the Bible instead of taking the infallible Word of God to search for the truth in science?

You bring up an excellent point. We should never use science and scientific theories to explain the Bible, mainly because science has not reached its limit. Even though we know a lot about how the universe works, we don't know everything. At the same time, we have to be careful about applying the Bible to science, especially when it comes to Genesis 1 and 2. This isn't because the Bible contradicts science (that is impossible, since the Creator of the universe also wrote the Bible). As Dr. Norman Geisler says, "There is no demonstrated conflict between Genesis 1–2 and scientific fact."

The real conflict comes when certain *interpretations* of the Bible (such as the interpretation that the universe is 10 thousand years old) clash with certain scientific theories (such as the theory that the universe is 15 billion years old). That's why we have to be careful about taking firm stands on issues like the age of the universe. The truth is that the Bible just doesn't definitively say how old the universe is. That's why we agree with Dr. Geisler that the age of the universe and the earth "is not a test for orthodoxy."

Is there an eighth day of creation?

I was reading the creation story in the Bible, and I was just wondering what your thoughts are on the eighth day of creation. Most modern-day churches are teaching seven days of creation, but clearly there are eight.

What you refer to as the eighth day of creation is found in Genesis 2. However, rather than an entirely new day, this passage is a review of what has been described in Genesis 1. Look at the text. Genesis 2:1-3 says that God finished the task of creation, and then He rested and blessed the seventh day. Genesis 2:4-7 then repeats (or summarizes) the entire creation sequence. The central focus in Genesis 2 is the creation of Adam and Eve, yet it is not a new day, since Genesis 1:26-27 has already told us about Adam and Eve.

Maybe an illustration will help. Think about describing a summer vacation to a friend. You might talk about where you went and the highlights of what you did. Then, when you think of a particular episode you want to describe, you might repeat a few of the details to put the specific incident into the proper context. That is what happened in Genesis. Chapter 1 gives the broad overview of all creation. Chapter 2 focuses on the creation of the human race with more detail.

Do fossils disprove the creation story?

One thing I have always wondered about is the fact that fossils have been found to prove that we were evolved from apes. They have supposedly proved the process of evolution from various skulls and bones that have been dug up, thereby proving that we have slowly evolved from the ape into the upright humans we are today. I am a dedicated Christian, and I have no doubts at all about how we were created, but this question has always bothered me. How is this explained?

Thanks for your e-mail. Despite what you've read about fossils, the indisputable fact is that no one has ever found any transitionary fossils between apes and humans. Over the last hundred years or so, anthropologists have uncovered fossils they initially identified as being links between apes and humans, but every single one of them has eventually been classified as ape, not human. In other words, all the fossils—including some very famous ones, such as the Lucy fossil—are of apes or other nonhuman primates.

Charles Darwin believed that man descended from primates, but he never had the evidence. He believed it would eventually be found, but so far none has. In fact, we have much more scientific evidence for a Creator than for no Creator (the basic belief of Darwinism). You don't need to apologize for your beliefs in the one true God, who created the universe and everything in it, but you do need to be informed. Read some basic books on the subject, such as our own *Creation and Evolution 101* or the excellent *The Case for a Creator* by Lee Strobel.

> **?** **What about the cavemen?**
> I am a baby Christian (four years), yet I seem to find myself in a leadership role. I have been blessed with a small Bible study group at work. I have been asked about the role of the cavemen in creation. When were they on earth in relation to Adam and Eve? I would appreciate your help.

The answer depends on your view of the timing of creation. If you take the young-earth creationist view, the so-called cavemen (Neanderthal and Cro-Magnon man) would have been created on the same 24-hour day as Adam and Eve, which was day six (Genesis 1:24-31). If you take the old-earth creationist view, the days of creation are much longer, and much more time would have separated the creation of the cavemen and the creation of Adam and Eve.

Both views agree on this: The creation of Adam and Eve on day six was a separate and special creation from all the other land animals—including the cavemen—created on the same "day." The Bible is clear that Adam and Eve alone were created in the image of God, meaning that they and all their descendants have the divine imprint of their Creator.

Dr. Hugh Ross, the noted astrophysicist, reports that some of the characteristics that identify human beings, such as religious relics and altars, date back only as far as 24,000 years "at most." Art containing "indisputable spiritual content" dates back only 5000 years. Therefore, he estimates that humans created in the image of God appeared somewhere between 5000 and 24,000 years ago, which is completely consistent with the dates of both young-earth and old-earth creationists.

> **? Does the Bible contradict science?**
> In your book *Knowing the Bible 101,* you state that the Bible contains no "scientific absurdities." What do you mean by that?

What we mean by that is that nothing in the Bible is considered absurd (or ridiculous) from a scientific standpoint. The Bible isn't a scientific book, but nothing in the Bible contradicts what science has discovered about the way the universe came into existence or how it operates.

If anything, science has had to change the way it explains the natural phenomena in our world. For example, until about 500 years ago, scientists thought the earth was flat. If only they had read the Bible, they would have seen that 2700 years ago the prophet Isaiah wrote that the earth is a sphere. You can look it up in Isaiah 40:22. Or how about this: Until a few hundred years ago, science believed that all stars were the same. Well, the apostle Paul wrote in the first century that all stars are different (see 1 Corinthians 15:41).

Here's one more that really gets us excited. Until the 1990s, most scientists believed that the universe didn't have a definite beginning. The general theory was that the universe always existed. Clearly this contradicted Genesis 1:1. Then in 1992, a satellite called the Cosmic Background Explore (COBE for short) collected data that proved the universe began with a single explosion of pure energy.

As you can see, at various times in history, the Bible has appeared to contradict science but only because science had not yet discovered the truth about the way the universe works. But God knows because He created the heavens and the earth, and He wrote the Bible.

? Questions about Noah's ark

For a number of years I believed wholeheartedly in evolution and Darwinism. I learned those theories in school, and my religious schooling was minimal. I still have some hang-ups with creationism—in particular the flood—due to my scientific past. How did one boat hold two of every animal in existence at that time? How did the human race and animals multiply so quickly and with such great diversity after the flood? How is there so much variation in ethnic and cultural backgrounds? Why don't we all look the same? And how was one small family able to repopulate the entire world? Questions like these trouble me. I believe in Jesus and believe He died for me and every other human in the world, and I feel guilty for asking these questions. I feel I may not be a true believer. I would greatly appreciate your help with these questions.

First of all, we want you to know that your questions about the Bible and the flood are normal. You don't have to feel guilty, because these are issues that are difficult to sort out. Honestly, we don't have any definitive answers, but we do have plenty of possible explanations. For example, one answer to your questions is that the flood was not universal, meaning it did not cover the entire planet but only a vast area in the Middle East. If this were the case, then people and animals would have survived in other parts of the world. We don't necessarily subscribe to this "local flood" theory, but some Christians do. It certainly is a legitimate viewpoint.

Your question about how two of every animal could have been collected on the ark is an excellent one. Even if the flood was universal, computer models have demonstrated that the ark would have been large enough to hold all the animals necessary to repopulate the earth after the floodwaters receded. Experts tell us that the ark was roughly the size of a current-day cruise ship. It had three decks (Genesis 6:13), giving it the equivalent cargo space of nearly 600 railroad boxcars. Dr. Norman Geisler estimates that the ark would have needed to hold some 72,000 different kinds of land animals (remember, the sea animals could stay put). Since the average size of land animals is smaller than a cat, the ark could have easily stored 144,000 animals or more.

And of course, Noah could have chosen to take baby animals rather than full-grown ones (this would have definitely helped with the hippos and elephants), and some animals could have been carried in their eggs. Taking all of this into account, the ark would have had more than enough room for the animals, their food, and Noah and his family.

As for all the races coming from Noah's sons, we don't know the circumstances that would have been in place in order for this to happen, but we do know that the sons scattered in different directions, so it is not a stretch to believe that the major races of humankind could have come from this beginning.

Keep in mind that we don't have exhaustive scientific knowledge, so we may yet uncover information that supports the biblical account of the flood. Recent geological studies have shown that a massive flood indeed took place. Science has no explanation, but the Bible does. New discoveries like this confirm the Bible rather than contradict it. This has happened time and time again.

Adam and Eve and temptation

Do we have any indication that Adam and Eve were ever tempted before the fall? Might they have made the right choice and resisted the devil earlier but fallen when he became persistent?

There's no indication in Scripture that there was a temptation or test prior to the one recorded in Genesis 3. God established one restriction and made it clear that any violation would result in immediate punishment. All it took was one act of disobedience for the human race to sin. It wasn't a matter of Satan wearing them down.

Are there other creation stories?

I've been reading *Creation and Evolution 101*, and it gives only two options about how the universe came to be. Either the universe created itself, or God created it. Considering the likelihood that the big bang theory is true, aren't there more possibilities? How about the creation story in Hinduism, an older religion than Christianity? As I understand it, this story involves one god who is eternal and several other manifestations that come from that one god. And what about multiple causes existing outside the universe? What if the whole universe itself is God? What if the universe is just an expanding cell?

We stand by our statement that where the existence of the universe is concerned, only two options exist: Either God created it, or He didn't. If God didn't create the universe, it must have come about by itself. Some scientists have floated two other options, but frankly, they require more "faith" than the God or no-God options. One of these other options is that the universe has always existed, but that is a philosophical absurdity. Philosopher William Lane Craig puts it this way: "Because an actual infinite number of things cannot exist, then an actual infinite number of past events cannot exist." Another way to look at it is this: The idea of a beginningless series of events ending in the present is absurd. In other words, everything that exists must have a cause, except for the first cause, which is itself uncaused. That is a philosophical certainty.

The other option (other than our two options) is that aliens from another universe brought the seeds of beginning to our universe (this has actually been proposed by certain scientists). Enough said about that.

Your comment about the big bang model is interesting. Yes, it is the prevailing scientific theory of the day, but it is perfectly consistent with the Bible's account of creation. Science now accepts the notion that the universe had a definite point-in-time beginning. Of course, the implications of that point to Genesis 1:1, so some scientists are reluctant to deal with the question, if the universe had a beginning, then who or what began it?

The idea that the whole universe is God is called *monism,* and that belief system doesn't deal with the origin of the universe. Monism leaves no room for a personal God because all is God. It's really more of a philosophical system of thought that has no basis in the way things really are.

That's the beauty of Christianity as a belief system. It's consistent with the way things are in the world. You don't have to believe one thing (such as a Buddhist denying that the material world exists) and then practice something contrary to your beliefs (a Buddhist assumes that the world exists when going about everyday tasks). The Bible also offers the only explanation for origins that is consistent with what we observe in the universe. No other holy book or system of belief even comes close.

As for Hinduism, it doesn't provide any answers to the question of origins. A hymn from the *Rig Veda* says that:

> He, the first origin of this creation,
> whether he formed it all or did not form it,
> Whose eye controls this world in highest heaven,
> he verily knows it, or perhaps he knows it not.

Hinduism doesn't really concern itself with matter anyway. What matters is to attain freedom from matter. The idea is to eliminate all ties to the material plane of existence and to understand how you are personally related to the spiritual whole. Historically, the two mantras of Hinduism have been "All is one" and "All is God."

When you deal with this whole topic of the universe and how it came to be here, the first basic question you have to deal with is, does God exist? If God does exist, then creating the universe the way the Bible describes is consistent with His capabilities and nature. In other words, with God, creating the universe is no big deal. On the other hand, if God doesn't exist, then you have to come up with a pretty good explanation as to how it got here, and so far no one has come up with any ideas that are scientifically and philosophically credible. Darwinism is certainly an option, but to believe Darwinism, you have to believe that the universe came about by itself and was developed through random mutation and natural selection, which means we are just biological organisms that came from nothing and will end up as nothing.

Whether or not that viewpoint is consistent with the way things are is a decision every person has to make.

Are faith and reason mutually exclusive?
I'm studying the Bible, and when I read Genesis 1, I can't get past the evolution of man, the ice age, and

dinosaurs—you know, the whole timeline in the stacks of *National Geographic* magazines in our bookcase. Genesis says God created everything, including time. So time starts then, right? And He made man in His own likeness, but there's no mention of prehistoric man or apes. Like I said, the whole timeline of science is nagging me. My buddy tells me to have faith, which means there are no answers to my questions. Can you help? Like I said, I'm studying the Bible and I want to learn.

Thanks for your excellent questions. First we want to address the issue of faith. A common misunderstanding people often have is that faith and reason (or reasonable answers) are mutually exclusive. That's not the case! Faith is required to come to God in the first place—in fact it's the only way to receive Jesus Christ as Savior (see Ephesians 2:8-9)—but the things of God also have a rational element. Faith isn't a leap in the dark. It's more like a leap in the light. Certainly we will never understand some things about God (after all, He is God), but plenty of stuff about Him and the universe He created is perfectly knowable and reasonable.

St. Anselm, who lived in the eleventh century, said, "I believe so that I may understand." He also said, "Christ must come to the intellect through the avenue of faith." Anselm was against blind belief and referred to a "sin of neglect"—having faith but not seeking knowledge. The apostle Paul was big on knowledge as well. He prayed that God would give the Colossians "a complete understanding" of what He wanted to do in their lives and that He would make them "wise with spiritual wisdom" (Colossians 1:9). Similarly, the apostle Peter encouraged believers, "And if you are asked about your Christian hope, always be ready to explain it" (1 Peter 3:15).

So we want to encourage you in your desire to understand the things you are first approaching by faith. Don't let your knowledge overshadow your faith, but rather use it to strengthen and support your faith. All of the things you are wondering about—evolution, the ice age, and dinosaurs—are completely compatible with the Bible and what it says about how we got here. The Bible may not mention these things by name, but the creation account described in Genesis allows for these things as long as you don't strap yourself to a single timeline for Genesis. In other words, don't box God in by saying that the beginning of the universe took place a few thousand years ago. (We know you don't necessarily subscribe to this view, but many Christians do, and that position causes problems when we try to reconcile the Bible with the observable universe.)

You are on an exciting adventure. You're going to discover some amazing things, and we believe your discoveries are going to draw you close to the God who created it all.

Chapter 7

Salvation

The Bible tells us that salvation is a free gift from God. That seems pretty simple and straightforward. But we receive many questions about how God's plan of salvation applies in individual circumstances. The situations in the questions below may be different from yours, but the biblical principles of salvation that we discuss are universal.

Is God fair when it comes to salvation?

An atheist friend recently challenged my thinking with this argument. If God is essentially fair, then every human being has an equal opportunity to be saved. From this it should reasonably follow that, statistically, every population group throughout history should have a similar percentage of its people who are Christians. Clearly this is not the case. In ninth-century North America, for instance, the percentage of born again Christians was very likely zero. Are some people weighted toward damnation simply due to the location and the time of their birth? How is this fair if we have no choice as to where or when we were born? Unable to answer this question, I am left wondering if God is inherently fair or if a belief in Christianity is even essential. My friend believes it shows that Christianity is merely a cultural phenomenon. How do I address this argument in a way that preserves God's fairness and doesn't compromise the Bible's requirements for salvation?

Since your friend is an atheist and therefore doesn't believe that God exists, his question is rather interesting. You might want to get to the bottom of why he would ask such a question in the first place. If God doesn't exist, why would he be concerned about God's fairness? Is he trying to convince you that there is no God by presenting an argument that would make you doubt God's existence? Frankly, that's not a very good place to start because even if you concluded that God isn't fair, you at least believe that God exists.

People sometimes apply the same kind of argument to God and evil. They will say, "The evil in the world proves that God doesn't exist because a God of love wouldn't allow evil." Many atheists use that argument. In fact, evil in the world points to God rather than away from Him. How? Because the existence of evil means that humans have free will and are able to choose between right and wrong. Only a God of love would allow His created being the choice between good and evil. A tyrannical and capricious god (like the gods of Greek mythology) wouldn't give humanity that choice. Such a god would create humanity with the inability to choose. In essence, such a god would create robots.

Now, your question about fairness is a bit different. You are concluding that God is inherently unfair because you know for a fact that not a single person living in ninth-century North America was born again. Okay, so we're stretching it a bit. But you did say that the percentage of born again Christians in North America in the ninth century was "very likely" zero, and that's pretty close to stating it as a fact.

Our only question to you is this: Where did you get your omniscience? Please don't take offense, because we know you don't consider yourself omniscient. We're just trying to make a point. When any person—atheist or theist—builds arguments on the basis of knowledge he or she couldn't possibly have, the argument fails to be legitimate. Where's the proof? In fact, the very notion of someone denying God's existence by using a moral argument (such as good vs. evil or fairness vs. injustice) is nothing more than a philosophical exercise. It offers no proof. In order to prove God doesn't exist, the atheist must begin with science. And make no mistake about it—the burden of proof lies with the atheist. The atheist must prove scientifically that God doesn't exist in order for his argument to be valid.

As you know, atheists have been trying to do that from the beginning, and they've been pretty successful at it—until recently. In the last ten to twenty years, science has advanced to the point where scientists are questioning some of the previous notions about origins. Darwinism (naturalism) has long held that the universe came about without God. It got here by chance, random mutation, and undirected mechanistic causes. Interestingly, scientific discoveries in the fields of astronomy and biology in particular have offered a credible challenge to that idea.

Dr. Antony Flew, one of the world's foremost atheists, has weighed the evidence, particularly in the field of DNA, and he recently concluded that Darwinism no longer gives us an adequate explanation for the origin of the universe. Dr. Flew is not yet a Christian, but he no longer considers himself an atheist. Being intellectually honest with himself, he has abandoned his atheism for theism.

This discussion of origins is relevant to your question. Your friend's objection to God's fairness or unfairness isn't a valid argument for God's existence or nonexistence. It's more about God's character.

On that notion, we would only offer this example. Let's say you knew a judge in your town who was presiding over the trial of a good friend of yours whose wife was murdered. The evidence against the murderer is clear. In fact, the person who committed the crime has admitted that he did it. All that remains is for the judge to impose a sentence. But rather than sentence the criminal to an appropriate penalty, the judge decides to let the murderer off, because in his view the murderer didn't really mean to do it. Would that be fair? Would that be justice?

In the same way, picture God as a judge presiding over humanity's trial. As a people, we have violated God's law. We have murdered, lied, stolen, cheated, and turned away from God. Does God have a right to impose a sentence? What if He doesn't punish sin and evil? Would that be fair?

In our view, God has every right to punish sin. In fact, if He wouldn't punish sin, He wouldn't be a just judge. God is just and God is holy precisely because He doesn't tolerate sin. If He did tolerate sin, He would no longer be just and holy. He would no longer be God.

Now, getting back to the judge in the murder trial for a moment, what if that judge handled the situation by giving the murderer mercy. And what if he did it by having someone else accept the penalty for the crime? And what if that someone was the judge's own son? It still might not seem fair to us, but what if we were the murderer? Would we accept the judge's mercy and his solution to accepting the penalty?

Of course, you know where we're going with this. The great God and Judge of heaven has declared us guilty because we have sinned against Him, but out of His great love and mercy He has decided that the punishment meant for us is to be taken out on His only Son, Jesus. Of course, because Jesus is God in the flesh, He is qualified to accept the penalty because He lived a sinless life. He is the perfect sacrifice for our sins. It doesn't seem fair, does it? Well, it's fair to God, and it's good news for us. But again, the choice is ours. God will never force anyone to do anything.

Regarding your moral question about ninth-century North America (or any other century or people for that matter), the short answer is that we don't really know how God is going to handle those things. We do know of documented cases of isolated tribes in the twentieth century who never had access to a Bible or a missionary or anything Christian, but they had an understanding of a personal God and His plan to save them through the sacrifice of another.

God tells us that we don't know His ways or His thoughts. He is God, and above Him is no other. Many things about God are mysteries, and that includes knowing how He saves people. As Christians, often we are too quick to pass judgment on who qualifies for salvation and who doesn't. We need to give God more credit than we do and trust that He will be completely fair to everyone because by His very nature He is just and holy and true. And we need to believe, as you pointed out, that God doesn't desire that anyone should not be saved.

We'd like to answer one more thing before we close. Your friend says that Christianity is a cultural phenomenon. We've never heard a statement like that. Frankly, it's a statement made out of ignorance. If it's a cultural phenomenon, then it has spanned 2000 years and has covered every single culture on earth. Right now two billion people in the world call themselves Christians. We suppose that's a phenomenon, and it certainly is cultural, if by cultural you mean every culture. But to say that Christianity is a cultural phenomenon, as if it were some passing fad, borders on the ridiculous.

We hope this helps and that God has given you eyesight strong enough to finish the reading of this lengthy response. God bless you.

? **Are we saved by faith or works?**
I am a Catholic who has been taught that what I do is what gets me into heaven, but the Protestant viewpoint tells me that I'm saved by faith alone. Don't I have a responsibility, once I have accepted Christ, to try the best I can to live an obedient, holy life? Why do the Catholics put so much emphasis on your actions while the Protestant groups put the emphasis on your faith? I have always struggled with this obvious contradiction and would like to know the Protestant viewpoint on it and/or how your actions affect your heavenly reward. Does this make sense? Thanks for any help you can provide.

Wow, you have hit on one of the major issues involving not only Catholics and Protestants, but your entire Christian life!

Yes, as a Catholic you will be taught that your works contribute to your salvation, but the Bible clearly teaches that God doesn't take our good deeds into account when He saves us. Read Ephesians 2:8-9.

The reason is that every single person who has ever lived falls short of God's perfect standard (Romans 3:23). All you have to do is sin once in your life, and you fall short. Because we are unable to earn salvation on our own, God sent Jesus to pay the penalty for our sins (which is death—Romans 6:23). Only by accepting by faith what Jesus has already accomplished on the cross can we be saved (John 3:16).

Now, once you are saved, yes, you have a responsibility to do those things that please God. The apostle James wrote that faith that doesn't show itself by good deeds is dead (James

2:17). This doesn't mean that our good deeds save us. What it means is that genuine faith will produce good deeds.

Go back to Ephesians 2:8-9. Now read Ephesians 2:10. It completes the thought:

- God saved you by his special favor (grace) when you believed (faith).

- Salvation is not a reward for the good things we have done.

- God saved us so that we can do the good things He planned for us long ago.

We hope this helps you.

Can you lose your salvation?

My mother was once a great woman of God. She is now in a backslidden condition. She told me that she has no desire for the things of God anymore. I understand that Christ died once for our sins and you only need to ask Him once to come into your heart. I have been praying Ezekiel 37:23-26 and Psalm 40 over her, and that God would restore to her the joy of her salvation and uphold her willing spirit. I pray that God would create in her a clean heart and renew a right, persevering, and steadfast spirit within her. I ask that God would use his Holy Spirit to woo her back to him. I also understand that she has free will, and it is her choice to return to serving God or not.

My question is, what will her penalty be if she does not return? Some do not believe "once saved always saved." What is the point of grace if you believe you can lose your salvation? Does she lose her rewards she earned when she was producing fruit? Does she lose the position she would have had in heaven if she had not backslidden? How do I pray for her? Do I pray for her to rededicate her life, or do I pray something else? As you can tell, I am a little confused, and everyone seems to have a different view on the subject.

About your mother and her backslidden condition, yes you should pray for her. Ask God to convict her through the Holy Spirit. If she is a true believer, then she is not in danger of losing her salvation. You need to understand that when God saves us, we are saved—forever. Here's why. We can do nothing to earn our salvation. It's God's gift to us by His grace, and when we accept that gift by faith, believing that what Jesus did by dying on the cross is the only way to be made right with God, we are saved (Romans 3:23-25; Ephesians 2:8-9).

Once we are saved, nothing we can do will separate us from God's love (Romans 8:38). Jesus said as much in John 10:27-29.

As for losing her rewards or the position she would have had in heaven, no Scripture supports that. We can understand your distress, but you need to give this situation to God. Don't take the burden of your mother's relationship with the Lord on yourself. This is between her and God. Pray for her, love her, encourage her, but don't judge her, and don't try to fix things. If she is God's child, she will come back.

Help for an unsaved husband

I am saved, but my husband is not, although he attends service every Sunday and loves it. Still, he won't get saved. I battle with this each day in my mind, and I pray a lot about it. What else can I do? Please help me with this one.

Our best advice would be to let go of this situation and let God handle it. You shouldn't have to battle with this each day. That's not your job. You need to trust God that in His time He will bring your husband to a point of repentance and salvation. You can't do anything to bring this about except to love and encourage your husband and to show him respect. And thank God every day that your husband goes to church with you and loves it. You could be in a situation where your husband didn't go to church with you.

Certainly you need to pray for your husband's salvation, but also pray and ask God how you can be a better wife to him. He may be resisting because he senses your anguish over this. Relax in the Lord and let Him do His work. You will be amazed at what God can do when you give Him your worries and concerns and trust Him completely.

God bless you and your dear husband!

Predestination vs. free will
What is your explanation on predestination, election, and free will as it pertains to salvation?

We will do our best to give you some basic views on these subjects. Please keep in mind that Christians disagree on these topics, and that's okay. We're not debating the nature of salvation, which is by God's grace through faith alone in Christ alone. Rather, these are topics that deal with how these things came about, and honestly, we may not know for sure until we see Jesus face-to-face. Still, forming views on these crucial issues is important because thinking Christians are concerned about these things, and it's good to have an informed opinion.

Our view would follow along the lines of Reformed theology. That is, we hold to the view that God, who is completely holy and just and sovereign, initiates the process of salvation.

This is based on the biblical idea that all have sinned and come short of God's perfect standard (Romans 3:23). In fact, sin has affected and infected humanity to the extent that no person seeks God (Romans 3:11). Rather, God works through the Holy Spirit to convict us of our sin and to bring us to a point of realizing that we need a Savior, and we move toward God. Before that, we're mostly running away from God. To repent of sins means more than being sorry. It literally means to stop going in the direction we have been going (away from God) and then turning completely around and going in the opposite direction (toward God). In our view, this doesn't happen until God works in our lives and gives us the faith to believe.

The idea of election—that God chooses those who will respond to Him—is a pretty big idea in Scripture (see Romans 8 and Ephesians 1 for starters). Yet election doesn't automatically eliminate free will. Even though God initiates salvation in our lives, we must respond by an act of our wills. The responsibility is ours.

Why God chooses some and not others is a mystery. It certainly isn't on the basis of good works, ethnicity, or geography. It's completely God's sovereign work. And God doesn't simply look ahead in time to see who will respond to Him and then elect those people. According to Ephesians 2:8-10, God saves us so that we can do those things He planned for us long ago.

Evangelism is still important in this view because none of us know who will respond to God's election. We need to follow Christ's commission to take the good news message of the gospel throughout the world. God is the one who saves, but we have been commissioned to be His witnesses.

If God saves us in this way, then Scripture is clear that nothing in heaven or earth can separate us from His love (Romans 8:38-39). The idea that we can somehow lose our salvation means that God isn't powerful enough to save and keep us. Honestly, people who wrestle with this issue— and believe us, a lot of people do—don't have a proper view of God's sovereignty. They believe that salvation is completely up to us. God is just hoping that we respond to the gospel, but He has nothing to do with our choice. Well, if our salvation is up to us, then probably we can lose it. But our salvation is not up to us. It's up to God. If He is the one who saves us, we can have complete confidence that He will not let us go.

Like we said, these aren't easy issues to wrestle with, but we're glad that you are. Don't expect to get everything down to a neat little package of understanding. Trust God for His perfect love and grace, do your best to work through these issues, and then be loving in the way you discuss them with others.

How do we know we're saved?

I have prayed many times, asking Christ to be my Lord and Savior. Sometimes I feel I'm saved, but on many days I don't know for sure. I sin daily, and I ask myself why I continue to do or say certain things if I'm saved! Could you please give me some insight on this?

First of all, we commend you for asking Jesus Christ to be your Lord and Savior. If you have received the free gift of salvation through faith alone in Christ alone, then you are saved!

If you don't feel saved, don't worry. You won't always feel saved. But you need to know your sins have been forgiven and that you will be spending eternity in heaven with the Lord.

Here are some Bible passages for you to look up:

1. Salvation is through faith in Jesus alone: John 1:12; Romans 10:9-10; Ephesians 2:8-9.

2. Once you have received Christ, you are guaranteed to go to heaven: John 3:16; 5:24.

3. Salvation is a fact, not a feeling: Romans 8:38-39; Philippians 1:6; 1 John 5:13.

Now, you can do some things to live a life worthy of your calling as a Christian. First, you should be reading your Bible daily. The primary way God communicates with you is through His Word. If you aren't reading and studying God's Word, you aren't going to be growing in your faith.

Second, you should be praying. This doesn't have to be a formal prayer but can simply be talking with God throughout the day. This is the primary way you communicate with God.

Third, you should be in a church. The church is the body of Christ, where all the members function together in mutual support and worship.

You might want to take a look at a new book we have written, a book for new believers. It's called *Growing as a Christian 101,* and it's available through our website.

May God bless you! You're going to do great because you desire to follow Christ fully!

What does it mean to be born again?

I'm just about to turn 16, and I've learned from reading the Bible that for eternal life, one must be a born again Christian. I've looked for books on this subject and tried to find more on it in the Bible, but I haven't exactly come up with anything. I've been preparing myself, improving myself, and adjusting my life to be a true Christian. I feel that I'm almost ready to finally be born again, but I don't have the prayer for it. I would be extremely grateful if you guys could send it to me and tell me if I just go about the process as I do with all my other prayers, or if there's a special way to do it. I don't know who else to ask; my family and friends aren't religious (in case you're wondering, yes, I do witness frequently), and besides, who better to ask than Bruce and Stan? I thank you guys again for helping me with my spiritual life with your very inspiring book (I plan to read more). Thank you.

Thanks for your e-mail. We are impressed with your sincerity and your desire to be born again. God is moving in your life and in your heart. You are on the verge of something truly remarkable.

There's no one set formula of words that you need to pray to receive Christ. What matters is the attitude of your heart. If you believe that you can do nothing to earn God's special favor and that the only way to get right with God is through His Son, Jesus Christ, and if you invite Jesus to come into your life, you will be saved.

Here's what Scripture says:

> *For if you confess with your mouth that Jesus is Lord and believe in your heart that God raised him from the dead, you will be saved. For it is by believing in your heart that you are made right with God, and it is by confessing with your mouth that you are saved* (Romans 10:9-10).

The reason Jesus is the only way to be saved is that Jesus died in our place in order to save us from eternal spiritual death. And because God raised Him from the dead, we can have eternal life.

Here are six foundational truths you can build your faith on. Read each truth and look up the verses in the Bible. Then you can pray the prayer at the end.

1. God loves you and wants to have a relationship with you (John 3:16).

2. You will never satisfy God's perfect standards (Romans 3:23).

3. Jesus did something you could never do (Romans 5:8).

4. The only way to God is through Jesus (John 14:6).

5. Jesus is knocking at the door of your heart (Revelation 3:20).

6. You need to personally receive Jesus Christ into your life (Romans 10:9).

Here is a prayer you can pray:

Lord Jesus, thank You for dying on the cross for my sins. I want to know You personally and live forever with You. I'm tired of running my own life. Please come into my heart. I ask You to take over. I receive You as the Lord and Savior of my life. Thank You for forgiving me of my sins. From this day forward, make me the kind of person You want me to be. Help me to do what You would do for the rest of my life. I can't wait to spend eternity with You. Thank You, Jesus.

Once you make the decision to accept Jesus as your Lord and Savior, we would suggest that you tell your family. They may not understand, but that's okay. Don't make it sound like you're better than they are. Simply share the joy in your heart.

Then continue reading the Bible just as you are doing. Ask God to open your understanding to His Word. You may want to go back and read the book of Mark again.

Next, get an understandable book that helps explain your Christian life. We have a good one called *Knowing God 101*. It will give you the basics of your new faith. Check it out on our website.

Finally, do your best to find a church where you can learn more about the Christian life, worship God, and develop some Christian friends. Since you probably don't have your own transportation (and couldn't drive even if you did), pray and ask God to lead you to a Christian friend who will invite you to a good church.

Be patient. You are going to have the joy of the Lord in your life, but you may also have some frustrations. That's okay. God is faithful. He will lead you in the small stuff as well as the big stuff.

May God bless you in your new life in Christ.

Can people leave God and come back?

Is being saved a necessity? Does it expire? Here's my reason for asking. I was saved when I was 12; I am 21 now and just now started to reconnect to God and religion again after about a six-year absence. During those six years I did some stupid things that hurt myself, my family, and (no doubt) Jesus. My prayer life never waned during that time, but when I wasn't praying I was drinking, smoking pot, skipping school, and disobeying my mother. I also have a brain tumor and have had 12 brain surgeries during which I could have died many times, but I feel as if I have been kept alive for a reason. God let me know in a not-so-subtle way that I needed to get back on track, and I have. The problem is that I have doubts as to whether I am still covered with Jesus' fire insurance. I have confessed my sins through prayer, renounced my old ways (actually, I find it nearly impossible to do the wrong things I used to do wholeheartedly and also relish in), and started anew. I plan on being baptized, and I will begin classes in September. I have also spoken with a friend whom I consider to be a very godly person and good Christian, and she assures me that yes, I am still good with God. Try as I may, I can't convince myself. Could you guys point me to some Scripture that would help me out with this?

Wow, you have quite a story! Thanks for sharing it so openly and honestly. We were blessed by the things you said.

No doubt you've read the story of the prodigal son. If you haven't read it in a while, check it out in Luke 15:11-32. The point of the story is that a son (or in your case, a daughter) will always be a member of the family. Once you were born again into the family of God, you became a member for life!

We know this is true because the Bible tells us that God is the one who saves us. We can't do anything to earn our salvation (Ephesians 2:8-10). And once God has saved us, nothing we do will separate us from God's love (Romans 8:38). This is very important. Just as we can do nothing to earn our salvation, we can do nothing to lose it. Jesus said as much in John 10:27-29.

Having said that, Scripture is clear that our faith in God is worthless unless it produces good works (James 2:17). That doesn't mean that the moment people accept Jesus as their personal Savior the good deeds start happening. It may take a while. Or, like in your case, you may do some wandering before realizing what it means to live as a Christian.

You have a wonderful testimony of God's grace and faithfulness. Like the father of the prodigal son, God let you wander. And like the prodigal son, you came back. As you said, God let you know that you needed to get back on track. But He never let you go.

Here are some encouraging words from Paul:

> So you should not be like cowering, fearful slaves. You should behave instead like God's very own children, adopted into his family—calling him "Father, dear Father." For his Holy Spirit speaks to us deep in our hearts and tells us that we are God's children (Romans 8:15-16).

We hope this helps. May God continue to bless you and give you His peace.

Are spirit and soul the same?

I have read through *Knowing the Bible 101* and *Creation and Evolution 101*.

I need some help. I can't seem to be able to pinpoint the difference between our spirit and our soul. I have been referred to 1 Thessalonians 5:23 and Hebrews 4:12 but to no avail. I am a bit lost.

Any help would be much appreciated.

You raise a good question, and it's one that theologians disagree on. Some, like Dr. Wayne Grudem, see no distinction between soul and spirit. He believes that "spirit" is another term for "soul," and both are used interchangeably in Scripture to describe the immaterial part of humans that lives on after our bodies die.

Other scholars, such as J.P. Moreland, see a distinction between soul and spirit. They believe that every living creature has a soul, including animals. In this view, the soul is what gives life. It contains the intellect and the emotions. When we become Christians, God regenerates our spirit. In other words, our spirit comes alive (Romans 8:10).

Either view is acceptable as long as we believe that some immaterial part of us lives on after we die, and only those who have been born again through the work of Christ and the indwelling of the Holy Spirit will live forever with God.

Why does sin lead to death?

One of the ladies in our Bible study is not a Christian. We were discussing the verse "The wages of sin are death..." and she asked, "Why does it have to be death?" My answer was that it indicated just how seriously God takes sin and that even one little tiny sin is enough to keep us separated from God forever, without Christ. Do you have any further suggestions for answering her? Thanks!

That is a tough issue for non-Christians (pre-believers?) to deal with. The real issue is that they can't conceive of a loving God sending anybody to eternal death. What people prefer is a God who will let everybody into heaven because of their good deeds or, at the very least, good intentions.

You capsulated the situation very well. The only thing we would add is to go back to Genesis and review the arrangement God made with Adam and Eve. If they obey God, they live forever. If they disobey God, they die. It was very simple. Of course, we know that Adam and Eve chose of their own free will to disobey God even though they knew the consequences. Adam's sin infected the entire human race, and his sin brought spiritual death for everyone (Romans 5:18a). God doesn't condemn anyone. As human beings in rebellion against God, we have condemned ourselves.

If that were the end of the story, then it would be very, very bleak. But God had a plan to restore the broken relationship and to lovingly take care of our offense. He sent Jesus, who didn't come to condemn the world, but to save it (John 3:16-17). Adam's sin brought condemnation, "but Christ's one act of righteousness makes all people right in God's sight and gives them life" (Romans 5:18b).

The thing is, God could have left us dead in our sins. He would have been perfectly just to do that. But He had mercy (not giving us what we deserve), and He gave us grace (giving us something we don't deserve).

We're not telling you anything you don't know, but it may help in further explaining it to your friend. May God open her heart to the truth of the good news of Christ!

Chapter 8
Living the Christian Life

You'll find some fascinating questions and answers in this chapter. Some people want to know why their lives aren't filled with more passion for God. Others ask how they can change from a life of sin to a life that pleases God. And some people are curious about the nature of forgiveness. What does it mean to be forgiven by God, and does His forgiveness apply to every sin you ever commit?

Does God abandon us if we abandon Him?

I had it once. I was a believer. Actually, I still really do believe, but I have lost the faith, if you know what I mean. I've lost the passion, the depth, the drive with Christ. I've yelled at God, and I mean really, really yelled. Horrible things. Bad things. Unforgivable things. My husband left and divorced me. That was four years ago. I've gone through all the other stages, but now I am going through the anger. Anger at God for allowing the only person I've loved other than my parents to leave me. I am totally lost in my world. Anyway, I don't expect you can help me, but I thought my e-mail might be a little different than your everyday, run-of-the-mill e-mail. I'm lost, lonely, searching, afraid, everything you can imagine. I know, I know, you'll skip to the next e-mail and push the delete button on mine. Not to worry. I'm okay with that.

Thanks for sending your e-mail. It took courage. We probably aren't qualified to give you specific advice on what you're going through, and you probably aren't expecting that. We think you're looking for some encouragement and reassurance that God still loves you and cares about what happens to you—and that we can do. Despite your circumstances, here are some things you can know about God:

- God will never leave you. If you were once a genuine believer, you are still a believer. You cannot lose genuine faith because God is the one who saved you. Read the words of Jesus in John 10:27-30.

- God has forgiven you. If you are truly saved, then you are truly forgiven. God does not count your sins against you. Read 2 Corinthians 5:19.

- God will continue to forgive you. If you have sin in your life, you need to ask for forgiveness. This sin doesn't affect your eternal standing before God, but it does impact your ongoing relationship with Him. Read 1 John 1:9-10.

- Bitterness and resentment are sin. You need to confess your attitude to God. He doesn't mind your frustration and anger, but you need to bring your attitudes before Him. Bitterness doesn't hurt God, but it will tear you apart inside. See Ephesians 4:31-32.

- Forgive those who have offended and hurt you. Don't wait for them to ask for forgiveness. Just do it. An unforgiving heart can feed bitterness. Read Colossians 3:13.

- Seek to restore your broken relationships. They may never be the way they once were, but trust God to heal what is broken. You may have to go the second mile (Matthew 5:41). Trust God to restore your relationships in His time and in His way.

- Forgive yourself. Your unforgiving heart may be directed to you. Self-punishment is the same as unbelief. If God can forgive you, you can forgive yourself. Read Psalm 32:1-2.

- If you are truly repentant, see yourself as God sees you—a new creature in Christ Jesus. Read 2 Corinthians 5:17.

- Forget what lies in your past and press on toward Jesus Christ. See Philippians 3:13-14.

We would also like to suggest that you find a local church where you can be around other growing believers. Pray and ask God to help you even if you don't feel like it. Oh—and immerse yourself in God's Word. The Bible is God's personal message of hope, encouragement, and instruction for you. You're on a rough road, but you're going to make it. God will make sure of that!

How do you live for Christ?

I'm a 21-year-old girl, and I'm a Christian. I gave my life to Christ three years ago, but I keep struggling with some things like jealousy, pride, hatred, and unforgiveness. I see Christians like me who are growing in the Lord, and I envy them. I want to change. I am determined to change. Please tell me what I should do to bring about change and how I should go about it.

Thanks so much for your e-mail. We appreciate your

honesty. We want to give you some words of encouragement. First of all, you were created by God to glorify and enjoy Him. The problem is that there's sin in the world, and that's what separates us from God. The real destroyer is Satan, who tempted the first human beings with the lie that God doesn't love them and care about them. Unfortunately, the human race believed the lie and turned its back on God. But God showed His great love by sending His Son Jesus to earth to take the penalty of our rebellion on Himself so that by receiving Him we can have eternal life. That's what you have done. You have given your life to Jesus, and you are now a new person. Your old life, where you were controlled by sin, is gone, and your new life has begun (2 Corinthians 5:17).

Now, even though you are a new person, you are still going to struggle with sin, and when you do, you need to ask God to forgive you (1 John 1:9) and to help you. Satan is still going to remind you of your past, but you need to claim victory in Christ, who has secured your future. As Christians, we are still going to struggle with jealousy, pride, and an unforgiving heart. But that happens because we choose to live our lives according to our old sin natures. We need to live our lives according to our new life in Christ, empowered by the Holy Spirit. Read Galatians 5:16-26.

You can do some practical things to live according to your new life in Christ. On your own you can develop good spiritual habits, such as reading the Bible and praying regularly. But you can't do it all on your own! You need others around you who can encourage you and hold you accountable. If you aren't part of a local church where the Word of God is taught, you need to find one! And don't just go so you can get lost in the crowd. Become involved in a small group Bible study. You will find others who have similar struggles to your own. And you will find a way out of your problems.

May God bless you as you sincerely try—with God's help—to do the right things.

How does forgiveness work?

First of all, I have to say, God bless you both, Bruce and Stan! I found your book *Knowing God 101,* and you answered so many of my questions in a way I could understand and assimilate. Imagine my delight when I found your television show, *Christianity 101.* Okay, having said that, I do have a question. When we confess our sins to the Lord and accept Jesus as our Lord and Savior, asking Him for forgiveness for all we have done, thus becoming a Christian, is that it? How does it work? When we die and go before the Lord for judgment, do we have to have a clean slate at that time? What about the sins we committed but forgot to confess? I'm almost 60 and have major CRS (Can't Remember Stuff). I'm trying not to carry over lots of sins until my day of judgment is upon me. I'm not talking about really awful sins here, but still I want to be right with the Lord. Do you get my drift?

What a great bunch of questions! Let's see if we can answer them one by one. First, let's talk about forgiveness. One of the central features of salvation is forgiveness of sins, accomplished by and through the work of Jesus Christ on the cross. Sin is what separates us from God, and we can't do anything to earn our way back into a right relationship with God. That's the bad news. The good news is that God loves us even though we are sinners. As Paul wrote to the Roman church, "But God showed his great love for us by sending Christ to die for us while we were still sinners. And since we have been made right in God's sight by the blood of Christ, he will certainly save us from God's judgment" (Romans 5:8-9).

The perfect life, death, and resurrection of Christ justify us before God. When we receive Christ as our personal Savior, our sins are forgiven. This, along with eternal life, is what is promised to us in the good news message of the Bible (John 3:16).

This once-and-for-all forgiveness is called "positional." Our position before God is secure because of Christ. But forgiveness also has an "experiential" aspect. Even after we are saved, we continue to sin, and we need to bring these sins to God and ask forgiveness. First John 1:9 says, "But if we confess our sins to him, he is faithful and just to forgive us and to cleanse us from every wrong."

You are responsible to ask forgiveness for the sins that the Holy Spirit brings to your mind (that's called *conviction*). Once God has forgiven you, you don't have to worry about the sins you've confessed to Him. Satan's ploy is to keep reminding you of the past, to make you feel guilty for those sins God has already forgiven. Have faith that the Lord has forgiven you and cleansed you.

What about those sins you commit and forget to confess? Again, trust God that He will bring them to your awareness. Don't dredge through your past, trying to uncover sins you think you may have forgotten about. Deal with those sins you know about, and then once you have asked forgiveness, move on. The very fact that you are so concerned about this indicates that your heart is devoted to God. If you were like the person described in 1 John 1:10, you would have reason to be concerned. But that's not you at all.

Thanks again for getting in touch, and thanks for reading our books. We pray that they will continue to help you grow in your Christian life.

? Are tattoos wrong?

Where can I find the answer in the Bible about having or getting tattoos and piercings on our bodies? Is it wrong to have them?

Since we don't have any tattoos or body piercings (at least none that we know about), we probably aren't the best authorities on the subject. However, we can give you one piece of general advice and then refer you to some Scripture. First, if you're still living in your parents' house (and under their authority), you should abide by their wishes. If they are dead set against tattoos and body piercings, respect their wishes and obey them. If that's not the case and you simply want to know what the Bible says, we will give you the main verse those who are against tattoos usually quote. It's Leviticus 19:28:

> *Never cut your bodies in mourning for the dead or mark your skin with tattoos, for I am the LORD.*

If you take that verse as it is, out of context, then it would appear that God forbids tattoos or any kind of practice that would cut the flesh. However, when you read the verse in context, you will discover that other instructions precede this one about tattoos. Among other things, you should not plant fields with two kinds of seed (verse 19), you shouldn't eat meat with the blood still in it (verse 26), and you shouldn't cut your hair or clip off the edges of your beard (verse 27). That last restriction would be a little tough if you're a woman.

Our point is that not every rule in the Bible (and in Leviticus in particular) is meant to be followed to the letter. The book of Leviticus contains many restrictions that were given by God in order to keep the Israelites healthy and holy (that is, set apart) for God. In those days, tattoos were dangerous procedures that could result in disease or even death (come to think of it, things haven't changed all that much). The other warning in Leviticus 19:28 was against getting a tattoo for the dead, a purely pagan procedure that was an affront to God.

Depending on what kind of tattoo or body piercing you want to get, your mark could possibly be a kind of witness for the Lord. Please don't get us wrong. We aren't suggesting that you get a John 3:16 tattoo on your back. But if you want your tattoo to be a way to start conversations, why not start the conversation with God? How you do that is up to you!

How do you spot a spiritual deceiver?

I am a new Christian who has been very blessed with meeting wonderful Christian people who have helped me on my journey. One man from our church has taken me and my husband (who very recently accepted Christ into his life and will be baptized on Easter Sunday) under his wing and is helping us along our journey of building a relationship with our Lord. He has given us both a copy of your study on John, which we are doing together. I am writing to you because I have met a lovely older lady who is a very God-fearing person. She has spent many, many years studying the Bible. She tells me many things that are very hard for me to swallow or even understand because I am so new to this. She said that she hears directly from God, that He teaches her and tells her what to do. She said she has a very successful prayer life and also helps out many others because of this direct link with God. She also tells me that Jesus wasn't completely human. She also tells me that the Bible isn't the Word of God because humans wrote it and have changed it over time. She did say that it has some truths in it, but they have to be studied and sorted out, which she has done with the help of God, her teacher.

I guess my question to you is, are there other reliable resources (other than the Bible) to find out and learn about our Lord? This lady tells me that because it was the Romans who put the Bible together, they left a lot of things out because the writers themselves weren't Roman and that there are many, many writings from all the disciples and about Jesus' life as a child and so forth. I get confused because on one hand, she does seem to have a direct line to God, but then some stuff she says doesn't match up with what I am being told from my pastor and other mature Christians. Help me please!

First of all, it is so good to hear that you and your husband are beginning your faith journey. How wonderful! We're so glad that you wrote and asked about the lady who claims to hear from the Lord. It's very important that you sort out the truth. Actually, there's not much to sort out. With all due respect to your new friend, we would suggest that you see her for who she is. At best, she is misguided. At worst, she is a deceiver. It's one thing for someone to claim to hear from God. But when someone claims to hear directly from God, and it directly contradicts what God has written in His Word—or what your pastor and other mature Christians are saying—then it's pretty serious, and pretty seriously wrong.

If you want some evidence from Scripture, here's what John (the same John who wrote the Gospel you are studying) wrote about people like this lady in his letter to new believers:

> *Dear friends, do not believe everyone who claims to speak by the Spirit. You must test them to see if the spirit they have comes from God. For there are many false prophets in the world. This is the way to find out if they have the Spirit of God: If a prophet acknowledges that Jesus Christ became a human*

*being, that person has the Spirit of God. If a prophet
does not acknowledge Jesus, that person is not from
God* (1 John 4:1-2).

John goes on to say that such a person has the spirit of the
Antichrist. (In John's letter, he talks about antichrists
coming prior to the great enemy of God talked about in
Revelation—but we digress!) You have picked out some very
specific things in this lady's character. She is definitely anti-
Christ in that she is against Jesus. And her understanding of
how Scripture came to be written is completely false. No
mature believer or credible scholar would agree with her.
Clearly she is combining her ignorance with arrogance—at
least as far as the true God is concerned.

This is a good lesson for you as you begin your Christian
life. People like her are going to come into your life from time
to time. We suspect that you won't meet many like your
older lady friend, but you will encounter people who will do
their best to undermine your faith. The way to counteract this
false teaching is to grow strong in your own faith, and the
way to do that is to continue to do what you are doing!

- Stay involved with your church. In addition to the
  teaching and worship, you're going to find that
  your fellow believers will lift you up and pray for you,
  and they will benefit from your spiritual gifts.

- Stay connected to the man who is teaching you and
  your husband. This kind of one-on-one (or in your
  case, one-on-two) discipleship is an invaluable way
  to grow as a Christian.

- Immerse yourself in God's Word on a regular basis.
  It's great that you are studying the Gospel of John.
  Learn all you can about our Lord and Savior, Jesus
  Christ.

Continue to pray and ask God to reveal His truth to you. Actually, He already has. The confusion you felt after encountering this lady was the Holy Spirit making you uncomfortable in her presence. As far as continuing a relationship with her, that's up to you. However, we would advise that you lovingly tell her that you won't be spending time with her. You're probably not going to change her mind, and she will only continue to confuse you and plant doubt in your heart and mind. You have nothing to fear from her. It's just that you want to plant yourself in nourishing soil, and that's not her! You and your husband are like new plants that need to feed from the milk of God's Word. Here's what Peter wrote to new believers:

> *You must crave pure spiritual milk so that you can grow into the fullness of your salvation. Cry out for nourishment as a baby cries for milk, now that you have a taste of the Lord's kindness* (1 Peter 2:2-3).

As you grow in your Christian life, you will move from milk to meat. All in good time. Meanwhile, we are so glad that you found the Christianity 101 series of books and Bible studies. They can be a great help to you. More importantly, you have the true Lord living in your life. He will give you strength, courage, and wisdom.

Does God love liberals?

I'm a new Christian, and sometimes I feel odd because I'm not as conservative as many of the others who go to my church. I'm afraid to talk around others at my church because I'm liberal and sometimes opinionated. I feel that if I express my views they may ask me to leave the church. It's like I have to hide my true self. Is there a place for me in God's kingdom? Or will I be ousted for my views?

Thanks for your e-mail and your concern. We know exactly what you are talking about. Yes, many Christians are conservative politically. But the news media has taken this to the extreme and almost always refers to Christians as right-wing. This is unfortunate because it communicates to the world that all Christians are ultraconservative, and that has all kinds of negative ramifications. The fact that you have different political views should not cause any division with other believers. The reality, of course, is that people can get very defensive and emotional when political topics are discussed. We doubt that anyone would ask you to leave the church over your views. If that's the case, then perhaps you need to look for a new church!

There is a place for you in God's kingdom, not because you are a liberal or a conservative but because you are one of God's children. You and your fellow believers have this in common, and that should be the central focus of your fellowship with them. Hang in there. Keep your eyes on Jesus!

How do you experience God?

When people ask Jesus Christ to come into their hearts, how come they don't experience God's immediate divine intervention? I have struggled with this for 12 years, and the pastor's messages never seem to answer this question. I asked Jesus to come into my heart, but I didn't experience God immediately. How can I know for sure that God has not forgotten me? I know that the vehicle for salvation is God's grace and not works (Ephesians 2:8-9), but why do preachers use scare tactics from their pulpits? All they do is make people afraid of God and cringe in fear. That is not healthy theology.

When you asked Jesus Christ into your heart, you did experience God's immediate divine intervention. When

God came into your life in the person of Jesus Christ through the power of the Holy Spirit, you were instantly transformed into a new creature (2 Corinthians 5:17). You passed from eternal death (Romans 6:23) to eternal life (John 3:16). In a verse, here is your divine intervention:

> *But God showed his great love for us by sending Christ to die for us while we were still sinners. And since we have been made right in God's sight by the blood of Christ, he will certainly save us from God's judgment* (Romans 5:8-9).

In a nutshell, Jesus intervened for you. He took on Himself the punishment you (and us and everyone else) deserved. That is the *fact* of your salvation. Now, you are asking about the *experience* of your salvation. Why don't you feel saved? Remember that feelings come and go. You aren't always going to feel married to your spouse (if you are indeed married), but the fact is that you are married. The same goes for your faith. As much as your faith may seem to be based on feelings, it is actually based on the truth that God so loved you (John 3:16), the fact that Christ saved you (Romans 5:6-9), and the promise that the Holy Spirit has secured you (Ephesians 1:13-14). One helpful goal for you would be to learn more and more about God in all three Persons—Father, Son, and Holy Spirit. Here is what Paul wrote to the Colossian church:

> *We ask God to give you a complete understanding of what he wants to do in your lives, and we ask him to make you wise with spiritual wisdom. Then the way you live will always honor and please the Lord, and you will continually do good, kind things for others. All the while, you will learn to know God better and better* (Colossians 1:9-10).

Don't expect others to give you the feelings you want. Take charge of your Christian life and live to please God. The Holy Spirit will give you all the feelings you need. As for preachers who make people afraid of God, you're right, that probably isn't healthy theology. When the Bible talks about fearing God, it doesn't mean we are to be afraid of Him. As our friend Chuck Swindoll once said, to fear God means to take Him seriously and do what He says. Honestly, the problem with most people isn't that they are afraid of God. The problem is that they don't take Him seriously.

How to find Christian friends

I am going to a new school and there are a lot of inappropriate things going on. I want to fit in, but I don't want to be dishonest to God. At the same time, I don't want to be classified as an outcast. How do I make good Christian friends?

First, pray and ask God to lead you to some Christian friends. God is the greatest networker in the world, so don't be surprised if you meet some very soon. Second, don't avoid being friends with non-Christians. Even if their behavior offends you, don't judge them. You don't want to participate—for example, if the jokes get coarse and you are offended, don't hesitate to quietly walk away—but you can show them love simply by being a friend. Remember that most non-Christians think that Christians are judgmental. You can change that stereotype by being loving. And don't be afraid to talk about spiritual things with people. You will be surprised how anxious they are to discuss matters of eternal significance.

Remember, God wants you to be a salt and light in the world (Matthew 5:13-16). And the only way you can do that is to be *in the world*. Just be careful that you don't conform to the world's way of thinking. Instead, let the Lord transform you by changing the way you think. "Then you will know what God wants you to do, and you will know how good and pleasing and perfect his will really is" (Romans 12:1-2).

What are devotions?

I have e-mailed you before, and you really helped me understand what being a Christian is all about. My best friend keeps talking about daily devotions. Exactly what are devotions?

"Devotions" is kind of a "churchy" word. We'll do our best to explain it. One of the ways you mature as a Christian is to study the Bible, which is God's personal message to you. The Bible tells you the things God wants you to do (2 Timothy 3:16). Another way to mature is to pray to God and praise Him for all He has done, to ask Him for help in your life, and to ask Him to help others. Think of the Bible as God talking to you and prayer as you talking to God.

As a Christian, your goal should be to become devoted to God, who saved you through Jesus Christ. Reading the Bible and praying are two ways you can be devoted to God on a daily basis. In fact, think of the word "devotions" as being devoted to God every day through Bible reading and prayer. You can have your devotions in the morning or in the evening. There's no magic time—only the time that is best for you to be alone with God, His Word, and prayer. It doesn't have to be a long time. Start with ten or fifteen minutes a day. Read the Bible for ten minutes or so, and then respond to God by praying. Tell Him how you're feeling. Ask Him for help. Pray for others. He will answer! May God richly bless you as you become more and more devoted to Him.

What's the best way to witness?

How do you feel about witnessing techniques that talk about the ways we have failed to measure up to God's perfect standards? I guess the idea behind this approach is to make people feel guilty about the ways they have failed God. I've used this before with mixed results. However, I'm a little surprised at the response I receive from my fellow Christians. They say my approach is too harsh and not loving enough. Any thoughts?

It might be that the technique you are describing works best with strangers or people you know only casually and may never expect to get to know on any deeper level. With friends, family, and closer acquaintances, this approach might seem a bit harsh. Truth be known, the most effective witnessing is a combination of two things. First, your life must be a living witness, the kind that invites people to ask questions about your faith. Second, if you are asked, you need to be ready to talk about your relationship with Christ in ways that people can understand. The apostle Peter puts it this way:

> And if you are asked about your Christian hope,
> always be ready to explain it (1 Peter 3:15).

There's something else to this witnessing thing. Don't approach it like you're trying to win an argument or convince the others that they are wrong and you are right. Peter continues with this advice:

> But you must do this in a gentle and respectful way
> (1 Peter 3:16).

Another thing to remember is that when you witness, you are likely only one link in a God-ordained chain of events that will bring someone to Christ. Rare is the person who is approached one time, hears the truth about Christ, and then immediately realizes his or her need for Christ. More than likely God is going to use many things—people, circumstances, and of course, the Holy Spirit—to bring someone to repentance and salvation.

We commend you for your desire to witness. Don't worry if people seem put off sometimes. It may be that they are convicted! At the same time, do your best to build relationships with people. As they get to know you and see Christ in you, they will be drawn to Christ in ways you can't even imagine.

Is it okay to judge other Christians?
What should I do if some people around me claim to be Christians but demonstrate anything but Christlike behavior? Those who are acting inappropriately make me feel as if I am being arrogant, but that isn't the case at all. I am simply trying to become a better Christian myself, and I expect them to be all they can be too. If we don't do our best to enrich our faith, what will become of our world? I feel as though I'm in an ongoing battle, trying to hold people accountable without being perceived as a holier-than-thou Christian or troublemaker. Can you enlighten me with some of your wisdom on this subject or give me some good Scripture?

You pose a very interesting question, and we're not sure we can point you to a particular chapter and verse. We can, however, think of two examples. One, of course, is Jesus. He was direct in the way He handled religious hypocrites (those who said one thing and did something else). We're not suggesting that you get quite as direct as Jesus did because He had the moral authority to accuse the Pharisees the way He did. But there does seem to be some precedent for doing something other than letting your fellow Christians get by with inappropriate behavior without saying anything.

Paul was pretty direct in telling the Corinthians that they weren't even to associate with anyone "who claims to be a Christian, yet indulges in sexual sin, or is greedy, or worships idols, or is abusive, or a drunkard, or a swindler" (1 Corinthians 5:11). "It isn't my responsibility to judge outsiders," Paul writes, "but it certainly is your job to judge those inside the church who are sinning in these ways." Notice that Paul isn't asking us to hold non-Christians accountable for their actions, but he seems to be telling us to do that with believers. The reason, of course, is that those who claim to be Christians represent Christ! Every time we do things that discredit Christianity, we do things that discredit Christ.

Still, this is a tricky area, and we really have to be careful about not coming across as holier-than-thou. Actually, Jesus issued a warning about judging others, mainly because we have a tendency to see the piece of sawdust in their eyes while ignoring the two-by-four sticking out of our own eyes (Matthew 7:1-5). The lesson there, of course, is that we need to clean up our own act before we can ask others to clean up theirs.

The other example we can think of that may explain the reaction you are sensing from others is a story we once heard from the theologian R.C. Sproul. Dr. Sproul was playing golf in a foursome and was pretty much minding his own business. He didn't even tell the others that he was a minister. Then one of the players unleashed a series of swear words after hitting a bad shot. Someone else in the foursome who knew Dr. Sproul whispered to the guy that they were playing with a minister. From that point forward, the game of the guy who had used the bad language went from bad to worse. By the end of the round he was spitting mad, and he practically stormed off the course before his friend asked him what was going on. The guy replied, "It was that holier-than-thou guy. He kept judging me, and I couldn't hit a decent shot." In fact, Sproul hadn't said a word. It was merely his presence that unnerved the guy.

Sproul's point in telling the story is that sometimes the life we live and the reputation we have will make others uncomfortable even if we don't say a word. They will accuse us of being judgmental or holier-than-thou when in fact their own consciences are accusing them.

We don't know if any of this is helpful, but perhaps there's something in here to give you a little direction or at least food for thought.

Does God keep His promises?

I was raised in a Christian home but never truly understood who God is until now. Your books have helped open my eyes to many issues in my life that I need to work out. The past two years have been difficult for me, but it wasn't until eight months ago when everything fell apart. I was suddenly hit with problems in every direction of my life, including work, family, and friendships. I've recently discovered that sometimes God allows certain situations to occur in my life. He was obviously trying to get my attention.

Well, it worked! My life has changed so much in the past eight months. I've developed a personal relationship with God. I even speak with Him on a regular basis. I never imagined that God would actually talk to me!

In light of everything that has happened, how do I know God will keep His promises to me? It would take a miracle for God to give me what He's promised, and miracles just don't happen to me. I know that God doesn't lie, that He wants the best for me, and that He loves me unconditionally, but how can I be sure that His promises have the same meaning to me as they do to Him? How do I continue to believe without any hope in sight?

The answers to your questions begin with the character of God. Because of His nature, God cannot lie (Titus 1:2; Hebrews 6:18). He cannot deceive you, and He cannot go back on a promise (Romans 11:29; 2 Corinthians 1:20). Sometimes it seems from our perspective that God isn't fulfilling His end of the bargain—that when we trust Him by faith, our life is going to be just fine. The only problem is that no Scripture makes such a promise! God has never said that when you enter into a personal relationship with Him, your life is going to be wonderful and turn out just the way you want. What God does promise is that He will see you through your trials and temptations (1 Corinthians 10:13).

One of the reasons God allows trials and tribulations to occur in our lives is that they help us to identify with Jesus. The apostle Peter wrote this to the persecuted church in the first century:

> *Dear friends, don't be surprised at the fiery trials you are going through, as if something strange were happening to you. Instead, be very glad—because these trials will make you partners with Christ in his suffering, and afterward you will have the wonderful joy of sharing his glory when it is displayed to all the world* (1 Peter 4:12-13).

So why even become a Christian? Where are all those positive promises? What good does following Christ do if you never see anything good happen? Well, the biggest benefit is that you have been delivered from the curse and the death penalty of sin. Those without faith in God through Jesus face the awful prospect of eternal separation from God. But you will never be separated from the love of Jesus (Romans 8:38).

Besides knowing that your eternal future is secure, you also have the help and guidance of God right now. You said that your life has changed so much in the last eight months. That's not a very long time, and already God is working! Don't give up on God just yet. Give Him time to make good on His promises. Your new life in Christ is a work in progress. You may not understand the good things that are happening to you until much later. The longer you live for Jesus, the more time you will have to see Him work in your life in ways that are truly miraculous.

Yes, it will take a miracle for God to give you what He's promised—including eternal life in heaven and a life filled with meaning and purpose here on earth—but that's what God does. He's in the miracle business. A miracle is merely the supernatural invading the natural. Only God can do that, and He will continue to do so, just as He has already done in your life. Our best advice is to read the Bible consistently and with a plan. Read God's Word with purpose, and pray and ask God to open your heart and your mind to His truth and the full meaning of His promises. He will be faithful to do it.

Chapter 9

Marriage and Family

One of the great things about Christianity is that it relates to real life. Don't ever let someone get away with saying that theology (the study of God) is all "ivory tower" stuff. The Bible has answers for real life issues and problems. Oftentimes, as the questions below indicate, these dilemmas and predicaments arise in the family setting.

How can we entrust our children to God?

My husband is a pastor, and we have four children, ages 14 to 22. I am having such a difficult time trusting God for them as they move through young adulthood, especially for our oldest son. He has a lot of problems, and we don't see much fruit of salvation in his life. I fear for him as he leaves home and does not seem to have his bearings. He attends church faithfully and participates in our family times, but we don't see the heart change that we long for. How do I function daily with this tremendous sense of concern for him and our other children?

Hey, we don't have to tell you that there comes a point when our children have to make their own decisions. You do all you can do—nurture them, guide them, provide for every opportunity, put your foot down when you have to, set limits just about all the time, do a whole lot of praying—and then they get to the point (when is it, 18?) when they have to be responsible for their own decisions.

Those college years between 18 and 22 are tough because the kids come under all kinds of influences. Even kids who leave high school grounded in church and the Word of God can sometimes question their faith. We've seen it happen again and again. It almost seems like the norm these days.

You'll never stop being a parent, but a time comes when you can't parent, at least not in the ways you used to. We've also seen parents try to keep their kids on a leash long after the kids should be making their own decisions, and that's usually not healthy.

If you've done all you can, and still your son seems slow to embrace your values and your faith, you need to give him room. He needs to develop his own vital relationship with Christ rather than living it through you. Some kids just take longer to develop spiritually.

So how do you function with your sense of concern for your children? You just do. You pray for them, stay honest with them, support them, and let them make mistakes. As Dr. Dobson once said, parenting isn't for cowards. He also said (and we think this is great advice) that you can't blame yourself when your kids make decisions you don't agree with. At the same time, don't pat yourself on the back when they begin making more good decisions than bad. They belong to God more than they belong to you.

Here's a paragraph from Henri Nouwen's book *Reaching Out* that should give you some perspective:

> The difficult task of parenthood is to help chil-
> dren grow to the freedom that permits them to

stand on their own feet, physically, mentally and spiritually and to allow them to move away in their own direction. The temptation is, and always remains, to cling to our children, to use them for our own unfulfilled needs and to hold on to them, suggesting in many direct and indirect ways that they owe us so much. It is indeed hard to see our children leave after many years of much love and much work to bring them to maturity, but when we keep reminding ourselves that they are just guests who have their own destination, which we do not know or dictate, we might be more able to let them go in peace and with our blessing. A good host is not only able to receive his guests with honor and offer them all the care they need but also to let them go when their time to leave has come.

? What does Jesus say about divorce?

I grew up in church and was even baptized at age nine. I never understood what a relationship with Jesus really was. I stayed in church through high school (for the social life) but did not live a Christian lifestyle. I got into alcohol and pornography and sexual addictions. I got married and destroyed the marriage as a result. I never did anything to fix it. Later I remarried but was the same adulterous person. Then one day my wife (whose husband left her) and I walked the aisle together and committed our lives to Christ. We finally understood what it meant to know Him as Lord and serve Him, and we have taught our children to do the same. I sat down with my first wife (who is also remarried) and explained to her why I did what I did, and I told her how sorry I was and that it was no fault of her own. She has forgiven me.

Recently I encountered a pastor who said that according to the teaching of Jesus, my wife and I are living in adultery and will go to hell unless we get a divorce and live alone. I spent my whole life always doing the wrong thing in every situation, and now I want to do the right thing. I hate divorce and never want to do it again, but I don't want to go to hell either. My wife and I are both very involved in ministry at our church, but this pastor says that God doesn't pay any attention to what we do for Him because we are lost. Can there be any truth to this? Can I know for sure that God will bless our relationship? Sorry this is so long. I am just looking for some peace.

After reading your e-mail, we would have to say that the pastor you encountered has given you wrong advice. We have to be careful about saying this because we respect pastors. They are called to ministry, and we are to pray for them and submit to them. But from what you have told us, you are doing what is right, and the pastor is out of line.

First of all, you are not going to hell. That is utterly ridiculous and a complete misinterpretation of Scripture. If you have put your trust in Christ as your personal Savior, you are saved and sealed by the Holy Spirit. You belong to Christ, and He has promised a place for you in heaven. Nothing can separate you or your wife from His love (Romans 8:38).

As for your life before Christ, your story is not unusual. Just because you grew up in the church and were baptized does not necessarily mean you were saved. Going to church doesn't save you. Being baptized doesn't save you. Only Jesus can save you, and He did when you and your wife walked the aisle and committed your lives to Christ.

Now, it's true that God hates divorce, but that doesn't

mean it condemns you to hell. Sin is what condemns us to hell, but when we receive Christ as Lord and Savior, that penalty is paid. There is no condemnation for those who are in Christ (Romans 8:1).

The reason God hates divorce in particular is because of what it does to marriage. In your case, the problems you described happened before you were a believer. That doesn't make them right, but it does put your situation into a different context. Many people have been in your situation, where your life was characterized by sin before you became a Christian. In an ideal world, it would be great to go back and fix your past, but that's not possible. Your past is past. God has forgiven you. We admire you for going back and asking forgiveness of your first wife, and we admire her for forgiving you. That is exactly what God wants you to do. But you can't divorce your current wife and live alone in order to fix the first problem. That is utterly ridiculous and wrong advice.

Yes, Jesus does teach about divorce (Matthew 5:31-32). He said that divorce is not permissible except for unfaithfulness. This does not mean that divorce should automatically occur when a spouse commits adultery. According to *The Handbook of Bible Application,* the word translated "unfaithfulness" implies a sexually immoral lifestyle, not a confessed and repented act of adultery. Those who discover that their partner has been unfaithful should first make every effort to forgive, reconcile, and restore their relationship. We are always to look for reasons to restore the marriage relationship rather than for excuses to leave it.

But that isn't always possible, and in your case, you weren't yet a believer. So your divorce, while detestable to God, is not the unforgivable sin. And God certainly does not want you to divorce again.

From what you have told us, you and your wife are

doing the right thing. You are doing what God wants you to do. Keep growing in your relationship with Him by getting to know Him better and better through His Word, through a church that teaches the Bible correctly, through prayer, and through your association with other growing Christians. The road won't always be smooth, but God will lead you as you trust Him.

How do you witness to stubborn parents?
Do you know of any encouraging Scriptures for someone trying to witness to a stubborn parent?

Keep in mind that your best witness will be your life lived in Christ Jesus. There's an old saying that actions speak louder than words, and it's especially true when it comes to parents. It's going to be difficult for you to convince or argue with your parent that he or she needs to be saved. What needs to happen is for your parent to see you showing the love of Christ.

The Bible tells us to honor our parents (Ephesians 6:1-3). In fact, this is the only commandment that ends with a blessing! As much as you are concerned about your parent's spiritual condition, remember that God is the one who will prompt his or her heart through the Holy Spirit. Pray for your parent, live a consistent life in front of your parent, honor your parent. God will do the rest.

About soul mates
I have a question I was hoping you could answer. What is spiritual bonding between two people who are soul mates?

Spiritual bonding is when two or more people are drawn together through the power of the Holy Spirit. All who are

Christians—that is, all who believe in Jesus Christ and have accepted Him as their personal Savior—have the Holy Spirit in their lives. They are all part of the body of Christ (1 Corinthians 12:13). As such, they have a natural spiritual bond. The apostle Paul wrote,

> *Always keep yourselves united in the Holy Spirit, and bind yourselves together with peace. We are all one body, we have the same Spirit, and we have all been called to the same glorious future* (Ephesians 4:3-5).

Sometimes two people can share a special spiritual friendship. A great example of this is when David and Jonathan shared a special bond of friendship. The Bible says that Jonathan "loved David as much as he loved himself" (1 Samuel 20:17). Their spiritual bond transcended common friendship.

So a soul mate would be one with whom you share a spiritual bond and a friendship that goes beyond the ordinary.

Caring for our pets

I have a dog that I love dearly but that has a neurological problem that has left him incontinent. He's a big dog, so his accidents are of greater magnitude. I have tried several medications and doggie diapers, but none have worked for him. He eats great and his attitude is still upbeat, which makes the decision to put him down so extremely difficult for me. I hate the thought of taking his life away from him, and yet I don't want my house to smell of urine and stool. My husband isn't happy about this situation either, but he has been very compassionate for my sake. I have tried so very hard to keep things clean and smelling good, but it seems that half of my day is spent cleaning and washing and changing his diaper. I can't just put him outside for the rest of his life, as the cold and heat bother his joints, and he would miss being around us. Does God have any words of comfort about this situation, any direction about how we, as our pet's caretakers, are supposed to handle situations like this? I hate the thought of me being responsible for taking his life away from him.

Losing a pet is never easy, especially one as valued and loved as yours.

Stan had a similar experience as yours two years ago. He had a 15-year old Welsh Corgi who was suffering in the same way your dog is now. Zoey (the Corgi's name) was incontinent. In fact, she had lost the complete use of her back legs. Stan even fitted Zoey with a doggie wheelchair, which prolonged her life six months. But there came a point when the incontinence became a real problem, much like your dog's situation. Stan consulted with the veterinarian, who said that Zoey would not get better but would get worse, and he said that infections were likely to set in, which would cause severe pain. On the advice of the vet, and after much prayer, Stan made the decision to do the humane thing and request that the vet put Zoey to sleep. It was very emotional and most difficult, but it was best for Zoey.

Now, we can't make the decision about your dog for you. Your veterinarian and you are the only ones qualified to make that decision (and ultimately it will be up to you) because God has entrusted you with the responsibility to be your dog's caretaker. The Bible says that as humans, we are to manage and care for the animals. We live in an industrial and not an agrarian society, and just about the only animals we come into contact with are our pets. So it is important that we care for them, especially as they grow old. This also includes being humane, meaning that we should not allow them to suffer.

From all you have told us, you have taken extraordinary measures to care for your dear pet, and God is honored by that. Your dog may still die on his own, or it may be your responsibility to help him in his hour of need. Either way, you won't be taking his life from him. You will be doing what God wants you to do.

May God give you His wisdom and comfort as you deal with what needs to be done.

God and relationships

Okay, here is my pathetic story—I will try and keep it short! I lived with and completely loved and adored my boyfriend of seven years. He cheated on me and then broke up with me out of the blue. He then took that strange woman on vacation with all of our best friends nine days after I moved out of our home while I was living in a hotel and wondering why we broke up! He somehow managed to tell all of our mutual friends lies about me to make what he did seem justified. He has not lost one friend from all of this. I have lost many as I confronted my so-called friends to ask how they could go on vacation with this woman. Nobody wanted to rock the boat and say anything.

My now ex-boyfriend admitted to all of this—and for a brief moment felt shame. He cheated on his former wife, he cheated on his former girlfriend with me (I now realize), and he finally did the same to me. I know this sounds ridiculous, but he was 97 percent wonderful and 3 percent really, really bad and cruel. He has the fear of abandonment from being adopted—he does not know anything about his birth parents. He is a giver to the poor, very kind to everybody, and very ethical except to the women he loves the most! That is how he charms people into still knowing him. He is a good man with an addiction like an alcoholic.

This horror story happened to me about six months ago, and I am still in shock from his actions. But almost even more painful is the way my friends treated me and stood by him! Your books helped me during the most miserable, sad, confusing, and lonely time of my life—especially pages 164 and 165 of *Bible Prophecy 101,* where you quoted Psalm 37:35: "I myself have seen it happen—proud and evil people thriving like mighty trees." And you wrote, "Jesus was betrayed by someone He trusted. Why should we be surprised when friends turn against us?"

It took me many months (I am still not 100 percent there) to make any bit of sense out of this, but this is what I came up with. Is it possible that as I loved him so much, and I would have never left him, that something so awful had to happen or I would have never left? He is Jewish and thought I was crazy for believing that Jesus is the Son of God...I just cannot imagine any other reason why this happened to me.

One other thing, the night before I found out, my body was almost buzzing. My eyes were wide awake, staring in the dark. I knew that deep down something was wrong—even though the affair was months prior. It was the strangest feeling. I found a love letter the next day. Could this be a guardian angel guiding me to the truth (perhaps a loved one?) or the gift of knowledge you spoke about? How can I fully and totally ever trust a man in a relationship again? This has happened to me twice, and I am only 33. I have been praying and thanking God for showing me the truth—and praying for trust and for the pain to go away. I also pray for this troubled man. Any advice for me?

Thanks for sharing your story. It seems clear to us that God pulled you out of that relationship. God's design for relationships is that marriage is the proper context for a man and a woman living together. The Bible makes it clear that anything else is not in His will for us. Even if your boyfriend had treated you with respect (which he didn't evidently), it still would have been contrary to God's will for you.

Can you ever trust a man again? Absolutely. But you need to set higher standards for yourself. First of all, rely on God and trust Him for your life. If you're not involved in a church that worships God and teaches the Bible, find one. Then find a Bible study so you can be around other Christians. Finally, pray and ask God to give you His wisdom.

You are on the right path. Stay on it!

The most important relationship of all

I have a question that I would like you to answer. You probably get a lot of questions on relationships...here is my story: I have been friends with a girl since we were five. We went to school together from age five to thirteen, and now even though we are in different schools we still remain very good friends. Recently I have been thinking a lot about her. I would like her to be something more than a friend, but the problem is that to my knowledge she is a not a Christian. I have been praying that she would become a Christian, but find myself thinking that I am praying for the wrong reasons. I want her to become a Christian, but I want her to become a Christian for "love interests." Is it okay to pray for someone to become a Christian so that you can get something out of it? Thanks.

We appreciate your honesty about your friend. First of all, we would say that you have your priorities straight. You know that a love relationship with a non-Christian is not in your best interest. However, having a friendship with her is fine. In fact, God may want to use you to be an influence on her spiritually. Pray and ask the Lord to give you wisdom.

As for wanting her to become a Christian so you can get something out of it (like having a relationship), nothing is inherently wrong with that. Your motives are honest. However, what you should probably do is think about what is more important than a relationship with you, and that's her relationship with God.

As you pray for her and talk with her, keep her highest good in mind at all times. That's what *agape* love—the kind Paul talks about in 1 Corinthians 13—is all about. Her highest good is to trust Jesus as her personal Savior. If you have thoughts about developing your relationship with her after she becomes a Christian, that's okay. But don't let it dominate your thoughts or prayers. Keep focusing on her eternal destiny. Love her the way God loves her.

Or to put it another way, your heart should break for her now before it melts for her later.

Can a relationship become a god?

In your book, you talk about not having any other gods. You talk about how different things can become gods in our life, such as a relationship. Well, I have just gotten engaged, and I wondered if you could give me tips on how to keep my relationship from becoming a god, especially in the area of marriage.

Yes, a relationship can certainly become a god in the sense that it can distract you from the primary position God should have in your life. This can happen in a couple of ways.

One way is when a growing Christian gets into a relationship with an unbeliever or someone whose Christian walk leaves much to be desired. Sometimes the unbeliever or immature Christian pulls the mature believer down rather than the other way around.

Or it's possible for two people, both of whom are growing Christians, to focus on their relationship to the detriment of their personal relationships with God. This is more likely to happen once the marriage begins and the kids come and the responsibilities of providing for your family and developing in your careers begin to pile up. This is when couples easily get distracted from loving and serving God.

Of course, this doesn't have to happen. Commit with your fiancé now that you will both keep the Lord preeminent in your lives individually and as a couple. You've probably seen the illustration of the triangle. Picture you and your fiancé at the bottom corners of the triangle and God at the top. As you draw closer to God, you will naturally draw closer to each other. Being consistent is not always easy, but it is so worth the effort.

The fact that you are concerned about this indicates to us that you will keep your lives in balance. Your marriage will be a sacred and wonderful thing. Your love for each other will grow even deeper as you grow together in Christ.

God bless you in your exciting life ahead!

Should we be 100 percent honest with friends?

I have a question about friendship. I have lots of acquaintances but not too many friends. I tend to be a loyal, honest, trustworthy person, and I am very serious and deep with my friends. In fact, one of my friends told me that I tend to be too serious. I got a little bothered by that comment because I don't think it is fair that I give so much of myself and get such poor responses from those

I really care about. My friend also said that I want everyone to be like myself, and I replied, "Why not? Nothing is wrong with being serious and deep toward the people that we care for." So I have decided to limit my sharing of what I have to offer, which is just plain love.

Another person (not yet considered a friend) and I were talking recently, and I told this person that he tends to talk a lot about himself—what he has or owns, what his future goals are—but that nothing is wrong with that because he is proud of what he has become and what he will become. I told him that I saw this as a positive thing but that most people might think he is showing off. He did not speak to me for several days, and when we finally spoke, the first thing he brought up was the comment I had made. He said I was "nuts" and "out there" because I sounded like I did not care. I assured him that wasn't the case, and I explained my point of view once more. He said that he did not get bothered by what I had to say, that it was no big deal. So here's my question to you, Stan and Bruce. Do you think that he was bothered with what I had said?

Friendship is so complicated and overwhelming... do you think it should be like this?

Apparently he was bothered by what you said. It kind of reminds us of the old saying, "Sometimes the truth hurts."

You're really talking about two different issues here. One is honesty, and the other is friendship. Certainly the two are related, but let's treat them individually for a moment.

As for honesty, there's another saying that goes, "Honesty is the best policy," and certainly we're not going to argue with that. However, there are times when honesty can be offensive. To use a supreme example, Jesus was very honest with people He met, and sometimes His honesty offended them (the religious leaders are a case in point). Of course, Jesus knew what was in the heart of every person, so we can assume that He knew the appropriate time to express His all-knowing honesty.

Above all, Jesus demonstrated love, which is the trump card that prevails over all emotions. Perhaps the apostle Paul summed it best when he said, "Get rid of all bitterness, rage, anger, harsh words, and slander, as well as all types of malicious behavior. Instead, be kind to each other, tender-hearted, forgiving one another, just as God through Christ has forgiven you" (Ephesians 4:31-32).

Another way to look at it is this: Would you want everyone else to be as honest with you as you are with others? It's okay (and sometimes advisable) to refrain from saying what you think about people. Just because you are speaking the truth doesn't mean you are doing it in love.

Now, as for friendship, you certainly have the prerogative to choose your friends and to be selective. You probably are wise to do so. Just keep in mind that you can have different types of friendships. Not everyone is going to be close, but you can have many acquaintances to whom you are kind and tenderhearted. We shouldn't be choosy about the people to whom we are kind. The goal is not to please people but to love them with Christlike love.

Hope this helps. We appreciate your candor. Thanks for getting in touch.

Chapter 10

The Church

With so many churches out there, how can you know which one is right for you? How do you know a church is teaching the right things? What happens when churches disagree? And what about baptism and tithing? If you want to be a Christian, do you have to be baptized, and does God expect us to give Him a certain percentage of our money? For answers to questions like these, read on!

Is watching church as good as attending church?

I have a question that has been bugging me. I haven't been to church in a number of years. I was channel surfing and came across a broadcast of a church service and really enjoyed it. It wasn't local, so I wouldn't be able to attend it. Is watching a church broadcast just as good as a real church service? See, my problem is that when I do go to church, I can't understand a word the preacher is saying. However, when I watched the preacher on television, I understood what he was saying and applied it to my daily life. Isn't this just as good as physically going to church? If you could help me, that would be wonderful.

You've asked a great question about church. A lot of Christians have given up on church, perhaps because of a bad experience or because they can't relate to what the preacher is saying. Maybe they don't like the music, or they might simply prefer the convenience of staying at home and watching church on television.

There are many good Christian programs on television (and some that aren't so good), and you can certainly get a lot out of what some of the preachers are saying. In order to get on television, you've got to be an exceptional communicator, so it makes sense that you can understand those guys. However, watching church on television should not be a substitute for actually going to church. Even the TV preachers would tell you that. You see, when you became a Christian, you were baptized into the body of Christ by the Holy Spirit (1 Corinthians 12:13). That means that as a Christian you share something that all other Christians have, and that's Christ in you!

God intends for those who are part of the body of Christ to be together, and the way that happens is through a local church. That's why churches were started in the first place—so believers could share with each other in all things, including worship, teaching, and prayer. Sometime read 1 Corinthians 12:12-31. You will see that each of us is part of the larger body of Christ, and we all need each other. You have at least one spiritual gift that some church somewhere needs. Pray that God will lead you to the church that's right for you—and that needs your gifts—so you can begin to do your part as a member of Christ's body.

Yes, you can get good teaching on TV, and you could probably even worship God by singing alone, but you need the fellowship of your fellow believers so you can grow strong as a Christian. And other believers need the gifts that you have so that the whole body can be strengthened. As the apostle Paul wrote, "Now all of you together are Christ's body, and each one of you is a separate and necessary part of it" (1 Corinthians 12:27).

The bottom line? Look for a church where the pastor clearly teaches the Scriptures, where God is worshipped, where baptism and communion are practiced, and where you can benefit from that teaching and the contact with other believers. Trust us, you will grow as a believer in so many ways!

? Why do churches disagree?

First, I want to thank you for your Christianity 101 books. They are truly a useful and motivating resource for me. I'm a new Christian, and here's my question: How can I best choose a church that has sound doctrine? I am now visiting several before I commit to one, but most churches seem to be in agreement 90 percent of the time, and then the waters become much murkier. What bothers me is that several seem to say their way is the only true way. How do I go about choosing the right church?

Thanks for your e-mail. We agree that finding a church that has sound doctrine (that is, correct teaching) is very important. The best way to evaluate a church's teaching is to know the truth yourself. Acts 17:11 gives us the Berean principle. The apostle Paul went to Berea to teach, and he commended the people there for being more open-minded than those in other churches. Not only that, but they searched the Scriptures to make sure Paul and Silas were teaching the truth. That's the mark of a mature believer.

You're probably right on the money when you say that most churches line up 90 percent of the time in their doctrinal positions. It's the other 10 percent (where churches may disagree) where you need to ask the Lord to give you discernment. Our experience tells us that the 10 percent area of disagreement often does not include crucial doctrinal issues but rather areas of preference, such as styles of worship and the way the church service is ordered. Here you need to find a church that is in harmony with your own worship style, but don't be afraid to open yourself to something new.

As far as churches thinking they are the only true way, the only way you can make that claim is to place it on Jesus. No one church is the true way. Rather, the person and the teachings of Jesus are exclusive. As long as a church follows Christ, they can make that claim on His behalf but not on their own behalf. Be careful of a church that sets itself up as better or truer than all other churches.

Hope this gives you some perspective. Again, ask the Lord to give you spiritual discernment as you pray and study the Bible over this matter. We're confident that God will show you the church that's best for you, and then once you find it, get involved! Don't just be a "pew sitter." The body of Christ (the church) needs your spiritual gifts.

How to choose a church

My wife and I are looking for a church, but we're having a hard time sorting through the different denominations. What do we look for?

Here are some basic guidelines you can follow for choosing a church:

1. Look for a church that faithfully teaches the Word of God. This is generally the responsibility of the pastor/teacher. Some pastors teach in a more topical style, presenting a theme or topic and then supporting it with various Scriptures. Other pastors

teach in an expositional manner, leading you through a chapter or book of the Bible verse by verse. Some pastors will mix up their preaching style between topical and expositional. That's fine as long as they teach the Bible.

2. Look for a church that worships God in a way that's meaningful. The style isn't as important as the intention of the worship. It should be to glorify God, not entertain the people. In worship, God is the audience, and we are the performers.

3. Look for a church that practices baptism and communion. Jesus Himself commanded that we observe these sacraments.

4. Look for a church that provides opportunities for you to fellowship with other Christians. Don't be content with just attending the worship service. Get involved in a Bible study, a class, or a small group. You are part of the body of Christ, which is made up of all believers. We are to learn from and care for one another in a Christlike manner.

As for the different denominations, that's going to be a matter of personal preference. Some churches are more traditional and follow denominational guidelines and doctrines, while others operate more independently. Any church you visit will have a statement of beliefs and probably even a history of the church and denomination, if it belongs to one. Should you decide to become a member of a particular church (something we recommend), you will probably be led through a series of classes explaining the history and the doctrinal position of that church.

Hey, we're excited for you as you look for your place in God's church!

What is baptism?
Quick question. What role does baptism play in a Christian's life?

There are two types of baptism in the believer's life. The first is the baptism of the Holy Spirit, which occurs when we are born again. Writing to the believers in Corinth, the apostle Paul said this: "But we have all been baptized into Christ's body by one Spirit, and we have all received the same Spirit" (1 Corinthians 12:13). This type of baptism is an essential part of your salvation. The second type of baptism is water baptism, which is the public identification of the believer with Jesus Christ. Your salvation does not depend on water baptism, but Jesus commanded that His followers be baptized (Matthew 28:19).

Do we have to be baptized to be saved?
I was just wondering, do you have to be baptized to be saved? I read in Romans 10:9 that "if you confess with your mouth that Jesus is Lord and believe in your heart that God raised him from the dead, you will be saved." But I also read in 1 Peter 3:21-22 that "this is a picture of baptism, which now saves you by the power of Jesus Christ's resurrection." I was baptized when I was a baby but not since then. I accepted Jesus into my life a few years ago and was wondering if I should get baptized again? I believe that I was saved when I accepted Jesus as my personal Savior, and I am questioning the need for baptism. But I have been reading a lot about it in the Bible. Can you tell me what you think and possibly give me some Scripture verses to study? Thanks so much!

No, you don't have to be baptized to be saved, even

though Jesus commanded baptism (Matthew 28:19), as did the apostles (Acts 2:38). People who argue that baptism is necessary for salvation often refer to Mark 16:16: "Anyone who believes and is baptized will be saved." But this verse says nothing about those who believe and are not baptized. In other words, it's true that those who believe and are baptized will be saved. But it is also true that those who believe and are not baptized are saved.

The reason we can say this is the example of Jesus and the thief on the cross. Jesus told the thief who believed, "Today you will be with me in paradise" (Luke 23:43). Obviously, the thief had no chance to be baptized, yet he was going to heaven. Another reason baptism is not necessary is that we are forgiven for our sins and justified before God the moment we receive Jesus Christ as our personal Savior (that's your Romans 10:9 verse). Baptism occurs later.

Having said that, baptism is a necessary part of our Christian experience. It shows we are being obedient to the command of Christ. It is also a public testimony that we have been saved. Paul confirms this in Galatians 3:27, where he indicates that baptism is the outward sign of inward regeneration.

Now, what about your baptism as a baby? That was not for salvation; it was a sign of dedication to the Lord. Later in your life, you accepted Jesus as your Savior, but it is not necessary for you to be baptized again. You are correct in your understanding of this, and you can rest assured that you are a baptized believer! However, you need to know that different churches follow different traditions when it comes to baptism. For example, most Baptist churches would not recognize your infant baptism and would require that you be baptized by immersion if you wanted to become a member. Other churches, like the Evangelical Free Church, would recognize your infant baptism and would not require that you be baptized again, even though these churches practice immersion.

Should we be baptized by immersion?

I have confessed to the Lord that I am a sinner and have turned from sin and accepted Jesus as my Lord and Savior, so how important is it for me to be baptized in water, and do you think total immersion is a more complete and moving way to be cleansed of sin? Some information I've read says you must be baptized, and other sources say that if you confess your sins and turn away from sin, and you have accepted the Lord Jesus Christ as your Savior, this is all that is required. I want to feel completely right with the Lord. I sure could use your advice.

On the issue of whether it's better to be immersed or sprinkled, there are churches who practice both, and both are effective means of baptism. We happen to think that baptism by immersion is closer to the original idea. The Greek word for baptism means to "plunge, dip, immerse." Baptism does not save you, but it identifies you with the death of Jesus (when you go into the water) and the resurrection of Jesus (coming out of the water). The way you are baptized will probably depend on the type of church you attend. If you desire to be baptized, make an appointment to talk with a pastor. You will be instructed on how they go about baptizing, and you may even be invited to attend a believers' class of some sort.

Does the Bible tell us to tithe?

My question is about tithing. I believe in tithing, but my husband does not. He says it does not exist in the New Testament. He does give, but he doesn't agree with giving 10 percent. I realize we are to give from our hearts and are under grace now. Does that mean we should give more than 10 percent? Would you please clarify the New Testament concept of tithing. Did it change from the Old Testament or not?

The 10 percent tithe is an Old Testament concept. It represented a tenth of property or income for the support of the priesthood or for other religious purposes. References to the tithe are found in both the Old Testament and in the New Testament, but mainly it's found in the Mosaic Law. The early church didn't support the systematic giving of a tithe, even though some appealed to verses like Matthew 10:10 and 1 Corinthians 9:7-10. But leaders in the church proved that the arguments taken from these verses were not valid. They emphasized freedom in Christian giving rather than obligation.

Our giving should be motivated by our love for Christ to support people in ministry and the church, as well as the church's work in missions and relief. The problem is that most Christians disregard any kind of standard and give embarrassingly little. We shouldn't be obligated to give a tenth of our income, but we should willingly give more than we do. The Lord loves a cheerful giver (2 Corinthians 9:7). Unfortunately, most Christians are too grumpy and stingy with their finances. We all need to get some cheer, be thankful for what God has given us, and give a lot more.

Do we have to catch up on past tithes?

I listen to ministers on television here in New Zealand, and I have learned a great deal from their teaching. In the process the Lord has led me to start giving. I am concerned that I have been a very weak Christian in the past. Do I have to catch up on my past tithes? Honestly, I can't afford this, but I feel as though I need to do something. Can you help me with this issue?

First of all, we're delighted to hear from a reader in New Zealand. As to your question about catching up on past tithes, our opinion is that you do not need to do that at all. Here's why. First of all, giving to the Lord's work should not be a matter of compulsion. Under the old covenant (the Law), tithing was required. But under the new covenant (Christ), we are not obligated to give. However, God wants us to give, and to give willingly and with joy. If anything, our giving should be greater than the 10 percent tithe prescribed in the Old Testament.

As for your weakness in the past, you can't change that, and simply giving God some money is not going to prompt Him to treat you any better. God already loves you as much as He ever will, and He always has. Giving God more money is not going to make Him love you any more. At the same time, as you get to know God better and better, you will want to do those things that please Him, and that includes giving to His work. Giving seems to be a reflection of our heart and our attitude toward God in other areas.

When you give, be wise. Don't just pick out a ministry and give them money without knowing something about the ministry and how they use your money. We are strong proponents of the local church, so we think most of your money should go toward the place where you are learning from a pastor who teaches from the Bible, engaging in worship with other believers, and supporting those who are doing the Lord's work at home and abroad. Your heart is certainly in the right place. God will honor you as you honor Him with your money.

Should churches raise money?

What does the Bible say about churches raising money and selling items? Didn't Jesus turn the tables over when He saw people selling things in His Father's house? I want to know how my house of worship can raise money to help with expenses without going against the Scriptures.

The Scriptures teach that we are to support those who are in ministry as well as the churches where they serve. Paul often thanked the churches for their financial support (Philippians 4:15). In fact, the whole Bible is filled with examples of giving to God's work by giving to the Temple (in the Old Testament) and the church (in the New Testament).

As for the moneychangers in the Temple, Jesus drove them out because they were cheating the people, and they had set up their booths in the Temple itself.

Should women preach in church?

I have wondered about something for quite some time now. Is it right for a woman to preach in church? I have heard mixed opinions on this matter, and I am sort of confused.

People have differing opinions about whether or not women should preach or teach in church. Many evangelical churches follow the directive of Paul in his letter to Timothy, a young pastor serving the church in Ephesus:

> *Women should listen and learn quietly and submissively. I do not let women teach men or have authority over them. Let them listen quietly* (1 Timothy 2:11-12).

When we read Scripture, we should always consider the context of any verse or passage, and that includes the historical context. The early church was comprised of Jewish as well as Gentile Christians, but the church at Ephesus had mainly Jewish believers. In their custom, women in church sat on one side and the men sat on the other. In the Ephesian church, the women may have been dominating the services, prompting Paul to request that they refrain from teaching so that the men would have a chance to teach. It wasn't that women weren't qualified; they were simply more eager to minister. In fact, Scripture tells us there were many women in prominent positions in the early church. For example, the church at Philippi owed its origin to the conversion of Lydia (Acts 16:14,40). Philip had four daughters who had the gift of prophecy (Acts 21:9). There were also women who held certain church offices, such as the office of deacon (a term that can be either masculine or feminine).

In light of the historical context, some Bible scholars see the passage in Timothy as an isolated situation that doesn't apply across the board. Of course, other scholars interpret the passage as applying in all situations. We would suggest that you pray about it and ask God to give you wisdom. In the end you need to worship at a church that is compatible with your views, but you should realize that there are fine churches where women have positions of spiritual leadership, and there are excellent churches where women are not allowed to teach adult men.

What is the right way to take communion?

I feel stirred to begin practicing communion in my time of prayer, perhaps as a way of renewed covenant living. I want to do the communion the right way, so how do I do that?

The tradition of Scripture and the church is that communion, also known as the Lord's Supper, is administered by a responsible leader in the church. It doesn't necessarily have to be an ordained minister, but the person should be qualified as a leader. There is no precedent for self-administration of communion. In other words, if you desire to take communion during your time of prayer, you would not be following the teaching of Scripture or the tradition of the church.

We recommend that you find a church that administers the elements of communion on a regular basis. Some churches practice communion weekly, while most do it monthly or quarterly. You should avoid a church that doesn't observe the Lord's Supper, as it is the mark of an authentic church, along with baptism and the teaching of the Word. If you are physically unable to attend a local church, a pastor or church leader would be able to come to your home to lead you in communion. May God bless you as you seek to grow closer to Him.

Should children take communion?

It seems as though every time our church observes communion, my husband and I end up battling over whether or not our kids should participate. He thinks they need to be baptized before they can take communion, and I think they should be able to participate if they have the desire. I hope you can shed some light on this important issue.

Taking communion is not a matter of age but of your spiritual condition. Most churches and pastors would agree that only those who believe in Jesus Christ and have accepted Him as their personal Savior should participate in communion. By this principle, very young children should not take communion because they are not old enough to understand what it means to believe in Jesus and accept Him as Savior and Lord. How old do you have to be to accept Jesus? We can tell you from personal experience that four- or five-year-old children are capable of accepting Jesus, but it really depends on the child.

It's true that most people who become Christians do so as children. So in the case of your own children, the question you need to ask yourself is this: Are they genuine believers? If they are, then it is not only appropriate but important that they participate in the Lord's Supper.

As for baptism, we don't think people must be baptized before they take communion. However, if a person is a believer, then that person should want to be baptized as a symbol of his or her faith in Jesus. Some churches don't baptize children until they have had a confirmation course, which may occur in the fourth or fifth grade, so a gap may occur between the time a child receives Jesus and the time when he or she is baptized.

In any event, taking communion should never be a battle. Either your children qualify to take communion based on their personal relationship with Jesus or they don't. If your children are Christians, explain the meaning of communion to them and encourage them to take it. Also, be aware that when taking communion—and this goes for children and adults alike—you need to examine yourself to make sure no unconfessed sin is in your life (see 1 Corinthians 11:27-29).

Hope this answers your question. May God bless you and your family!

When baby Christians attack

First of all, I consider myself to be a spiritually mature Christian, even though it took a lot for me to let go of the past and totally surrender to God and let Him lead. Last year I took a spiritual gifts test and discovered that my spiritual gifts are discernment of spirits, prophecy, hospitality, and music. Before the tests people would always wonder why I would somehow know when someone was a phony in church. Most of the time I feel blessed, but I have found that I am under constant attack from the devil, mostly through unsaved people and baby Christians. I get so frustrated with this part of it. Is this normal for me to go through this in the church, and how do I deal with it? I don't want to lose or abuse my gifts.

Yes, someone with your giftedness can be expected to be under spiritual attack. It could also come as a result of jealousy or because people don't understand you. At the same time, you probably can take some of the pressure off yourself by developing another mark of spirituality, and that's grace. The temptation for people with multiple spiritual gifts is to appear super-spiritual. Even without intending to do so or without realizing it, you may be intimidating people, including your pastor. Back off just a bit and have an attitude of graciousness and love. Always do what's best for others. If you are dealing with new Christians or seekers, don't automatically try to show them how much you know. Show them your love and compassion first. Your knowledge will come out in due time.

How to deal with a hypocrite

I'm a teenager, and I have purchased one of your books. I've been reading it and discovered it's pretty good, but I have a question. You wrote about hypocrites and gave some examples. But what if the person was being hypocritical in a different way? I have a friend who is nice to me at one moment and then different with me at another. I've kind of had problems with this person, and I've been praying about it, but I need some advice. Please get back to me ASAP.

That's a great question, and it doesn't have an easy answer. The fact is that the church does have its share of hypocrites—that is, people who say one thing and then do or say something else. How do you deal with them? Try to understand that even though God has saved us, we are still imperfect people. Nobody is exempt from hypocrisy. We all want to put on our best face for others even though we may say hurtful things behind their backs.

The first person we should pay attention to is ourselves. We need to ask God to help us be consistent in our thought life, in our actions, and in the things we say to people, both in front of them and when they are not around. Jesus taught that we are to love others the way we love ourselves (Matthew 22:39). And we are to treat others the way we would want them to treat us. It's impossible to follow these commands and act in a hypocritical manner toward others. The other thing is to live out what we believe. It doesn't do any good to believe something and then not act on it. Here's what the Bible says about it:

> For if you just listen and don't obey, it is like looking at your face in a mirror but doing nothing to improve your appearance. You see yourself, walk away, and forget what you look like. But if you keep looking steadily into God's perfect law—the law that sets you free—and if you do what it says and don't forget what you heard, then God will bless you for doing it (James 1:23-25).

When you encounter others who are hypocritical, pray for them. Understand that hypocrisy comes from weakness, not strength. And if your friends are nice one moment and not at another time, compliment them when they are nice and refuse to be drawn into their negative attitudes when they aren't.

Chapter 11

Prayer

Imagine being able to communicate directly with the Almighty Creator of the universe! What a privilege! But it is a little intimidating. Judging by the questions that we received, people obviously take praying seriously, and they don't want to do it incorrectly. They have questions about the words they say and the motivations behind their prayers.

Who should we pray to—God or Jesus?

Who is the Holy Spirit? Is it God or Jesus? And when I pray, do I pray to God or to Jesus? If I talk to Jesus, does He go to God? I'm confused. I'm afraid I'm not praying right.

The Holy Spirit is the third Person in the Godhead. God is one being in three Persons—Father, Son, and Holy Spirit. This is known as the Trinity. These aren't three separate Gods but rather three Persons functioning together in perfect harmony. Each one is completely God. The Father is God, the Son is God, and the Holy Spirit is God.

When you were saved, God the Father reached out to you through Christ. Jesus accomplished your salvation, and the Holy Spirit applies it. The Holy Spirit is Christ living in you.

You are praying right. Don't worry. God hears your prayers regardless of how you picture Him or how you talk to Him. But if you want to pray "with the grain," then pray to God in the name of Jesus and in the power of the Holy Spirit.

May God bless you as you seek to know Him better.

? Can you pray to the Trinity?

My friend always starts her prayers with "Dear Father, Son, and Holy Spirit," and this bothers me. It seems to me, we should pray to the Father, through the Holy Spirit, asking for Jesus' sake. But then I think, why should it matter? Perhaps this notion of mine is purely petty. Yet each time I hear her, these thoughts occur again. Am I being petty, or is there a biblical basis for my discomfort?

Your question about prayer is common. Those of us who have been brought up in traditional churches have been taught to pray to the Father in the name of Jesus, as you said. However, we don't know of any Scripture that gives the exact template as to how we should pray. Certainly the model prayer (the Lord's Prayer) that Jesus gave His disciples indicates that we should pray to the Father, but there's nothing wrong with praying to Jesus.

It all comes down to an understanding of God in three Persons, which is the Trinity, and that's not an easy concept to grasp. We dealt with the Trinity on one of the episodes of our television show, *Christianity 101*. Dr. Fred Sanders, a theologian friend of ours, explained prayer the way you understand it: to the Father, through the Son, in the Holy Spirit.

At the same time, Dr. Sanders sees nothing wrong with praying to Jesus or to the Trinity for that matter, as your friend does. In fact, something is very biblical about praying to all three Persons. Your friend has a sense of all three Persons, and that is wonderful.

How should we pray?

How do I receive all the blessings God has planned for me, and how do I speak with God as I would speak to another person?

To receive God's blessings, you must learn to please God and honor Him in all you do. Read Colossians 1:9-10. God saved you by His special favor so you could do the good things He planned for you long ago (Ephesians 2:8-10).

God's blessings are mostly spiritual. When you live in the power of the Holy Spirit and allow Him to control your life, He will produce His fruit in your life (Galatians 5:22-23).

Yes, you can talk with God as you would any person. God is your Creator and your Father. You don't need formal words. Just talk to Him. Give Him your praise. Ask for His forgiveness of your sins. Pray for others. Tell Him your fears and your hopes. Ask Him to give you spiritual wisdom.

How long should we pray?

My son is a 23-year-old alcoholic. Severe. We have tried everything, including treatment centers. He gets violently ill when he has no liquor. He chooses to drink. God gave him a handsome face and a great body—he even modeled for a while. But he is a mess. Obviously I have prayed hard and long. How does one accept things when God says no to your prayer, especially prayer for your child? What should I do?

Our hearts ache for your situation with your son. Alcoholism is a terrible disease, and even people who faithfully seek treatment can have a difficult time.

May we offer these words of encouragement for you. As his mother, you are going to feel the pain that comes from having a wayward child. At the same time, your son is living his own life. He is making his own decisions, although at this point he is not going to conquer his addiction on his own. Professional treatment is his only hope.

All you can do is love your son and continue to pray. Despite this terrible situation, God is still in control. We can't always understand why things happen the way they do, but that doesn't mean that God is not hearing your prayers.

We can easily get discouraged when things don't happen according to our timetable. Sometimes God takes longer for reasons we see later.

Keep trusting God. Keep praying. God will answer.

May God give you strength for your difficult journey. And may God heal your son.

? Can our prayers create confusion?

I have been praying for a girl at work who will be leaving soon. I have been asking God to use me to be a blessing in her life and to keep me open to His will regarding how He wants to use me.

My main prayer for her has been that the Holy Spirit would open her heart to Jesus.

Guys, here is the thing—since I have been praying for her, she has started reacting to me in confusing ways at times.

Is the power of prayer so strong that the Lord is helping her to see something in me?

Please respond to this because God does put her on my heart very heavily at times.

You are discovering firsthand that prayer is indeed a powerful thing. Here's what the Bible says:

> *The earnest prayer of a righteous person has great power and wonderful results* (James 5:16).

As you are earnestly praying for her, God is answering. The Holy Spirit is responding and opening her heart to Jesus. Now, her response to that prompting could take many forms—joy, restlessness, guilt…Remember that when anyone is confronted with Jesus for the first time, or for the first time in a long while, the response isn't always positive. But there is a response. Trust God that He will work in her heart, but don't expect it to happen according to your timetable (we always want things to happen quickly). If her heart remains open, God will continue to move in His time.

The fact that your heart is heavy indicates that you are sincere and persistent in your prayers. Prayer is not and should not be easy. Remember how Jesus prayed in the Garden of Gethsemane? He was anguished. When He prayed for Jerusalem, His heart was heavy. Accept your own concern for her as God's hand upon you. He has willed that you pray for her, and you are responding. Hang in there!

? Does prayer change God?

I feel like a ten-year-old asking this basic question, but the more I read and learn, the more I question, the more I pray, the more I get confused. Does prayer change God's mind?

That's actually a pretty sophisticated question. We don't know how this "changing the mind of God" deal works. Nobody does. But this mystery involves the concept of God knowing everything (omniscience). Before the world was created, He knew everything that would happen in our lives. He knows what we will be praying about before we even utter the words. So do our prayers really change what God is going to do if He has known all along that He would be doing what we prayed for?

The truth is that prayer invokes God's involvement in the circumstances of your life. Yes, that's right, you can get God "on your side" through prayer, and He can really make things happen. But don't take our word for it; look at these true-life examples from the Bible:

- Jonah offered a panic prayer as he was getting an inside view of a fish's digestive tract. God caused the fish to regurgitate Jonah on the beach (Jonah 2:7-10).

- Elijah had a bed-and-breakfast arrangement with a widow in Zarephath. When her son died, Elijah asked God to restore the boy's life. That's exactly what happened (1 Kings 17:8-24). And such incidents weren't limited to the Old Testament. The apostle Peter also prayed over a corpse, and the woman came back to life (Acts 9:36-41).

- In what was a cultural disgrace, Hannah couldn't get pregnant. In response to her specific and fervent prayers for a son, she later gave birth to Samuel, whose name means "heard by God" (1 Samuel 1:1-20).

- In what must be every weatherman's dream, God caused a drought when Elijah predicted one, and it didn't rain again until years later when Elijah prayed for it (1 Kings 17–18).

- On the night before his trial, Peter was in prison, chained between two guards. A prayer meeting was going on for him in the same town. In the middle of the night, an angel appeared in his cell. His chains fell off, and the angel escorted Peter out of the prison without anybody noticing (Acts 12:5-11).

We can take great comfort in the fact that one of God's attributes is that He never changes. His love and His concern for us are unwaivering. And our prayers get God involved in the details of our lives.

Hope this helps a little. Thanks again for getting in touch.

Does God answer prayers of unbelievers?

In your books you write that if you're not a Christian, God does not answer your prayers. I just wanted to tell you that the reason that I'm a Christian today is because God answered my prayer. I believe that's one way God softens our hearts so that we will follow Him. I just thought you'd want to know I thought that.

You make a good point. We probably didn't make this clear enough, but there is one prayer God answers, and that's a prayer from someone who wants to know God personally. Hebrews 11:6 tells us that God rewards those who sincerely seek Him. In the book of Acts, Cornelius was devoting himself to prayer as he was seeking the one true God (Acts 10:2). God heard his prayer and sent Peter to give him the good news message about Jesus.

Yes, God works through the Holy Spirit to prepare our hearts to receive His message. And He hears the prayers of those who want to know Him personally.

Chapter 12
God's Will

A common theme in many questions we receive relates to finding God's will. Nothing is more appropriate than loving God and wanting to follow His plan for your life. But how do you know what choice He wants you to make? The Bible isn't clear on personal specifics (as in the best career choice, choosing a spouse, or deciding whether to wear solids, stripes, or plaids). But the Bible has definite guidelines that we can follow for staying within God's will.

How do we receive God's guidance?
I am trying to make a career decision right now. How can I know what path God wants me to take? I have read *The Purpose-Driven Life* and am trying to follow God's plan for me, but I have no idea which way to go. I have read the Bible, prayed, meditated, and listened, but I don't seem to be getting a clear message from Him. Any suggestions would be appreciated.

Knowing which way God wants you to go can sometimes be a challenging experience. And we will be the first ones to tell you that what you're experiencing is pretty normal. It isn't that God deliberately tries to keep His will from us. As you know firsthand, He has given us plenty of tools to help us make decisions—His Word, prayer, books. Still, we don't always know for sure what to do next, and sometimes we don't have any idea!

Here are a couple of suggestions. You've probably already done this, but it's always helpful to get the counsel of wise and godly people. Sometimes you're so close to your own situation that you can't see yourself objectively. That's why you need other people, especially people who know you, to give you their ideas. That's not to say that you have to do what others say, but definitely factor their perspective into your decisions. God will use the advice of others who are tuned in to Him to guide you in your decision.

Also, you may be worrying too much about failure. Sometimes the fear of failure can paralyze us, causing us to stand still when we should be moving forward. Remember, something is worse than failure, and that's not trying at all. Now, we're not suggesting that you go out with the mind-set that you're going to fail. You need to trust God in your decisions and believe that He always has your best interest in mind, and sometimes His best interest includes hard life lessons that come from failure.

You are doing the right things. Trust God to do His part.

? How can we know we're in God's will?

I'm a newborn Christian, and I just can't seem to find a fulfilling answer to this question: How do I know I'm doing God's will in my life if I'm not sure I'm sensitive to His presence (the Holy Spirit, that is)? I know in my heart that I want to go to college to study psychology, and different parts of Scripture say that if we're doing things that are not His divine will for us, those things will be in vain. I've prayed many times before, but I just think I'm not being sensitive to Him since I'm still in a dilemma over this issue. I want to be obedient to Him, but I don't know if just continuing this path I've chosen is what He wants for me. Can you help out?

Anyone who is following Christ should want to do His will, so we applaud you for wanting to do just that. However, that doesn't mean discovering what God wants you to do is going to be easy. Living the Christian life is a journey, and we don't always know the specific paths that journey is going to take. We know the final destination, but we don't always know what lies around the next bend.

You can do some things to better discern God's will for your life, but ultimately you need to trust God by faith to lead you where He wants you.

You asked about studying psychology in college. If this is something you desire to do, then here's what we would suggest:

- Pray about it. Ask God to lead you along the right path and to give you His peace that you're doing the right thing.

- Stay focused on God's Word. You probably won't find specific verses that will tell you what to do, but you will allow the Holy Spirit to minister to you and give you wisdom.

- Seek the wise counsel of mature believers who know you well.

- Do your homework. If you have chosen a certain school to study psychology, make sure you know what you're getting yourself into. If you are planning to study at a secular college or university, you need to know that the worldview of most of the professors you will encounter is against God. If you want our advice, we would suggest studying at a Christian college with a good reputation for psychology.

Even after all of that, you still may have some doubts, but some of those doubts may be there because you think there is one specific thing God wants you to do, and if you don't find it, you're going to be a spiritual failure. Remember that God created you for a purpose—to glorify Him—but He has also created you with certain gifts and talents. Use these for His glory, but don't get caught up in the notion that you need specific signs pointing you to a specific place. Trust God to guide you and then use your own judgment to make decisions—as long as your judgment is based on your growing relationship with God.

We hope this helps you. May God bless and guide you as you consider your future.

The Holy Spirit and our conscience

How can you distinguish between the Holy Spirit and your conscience, between doing what you think is right and safe and listening to the voice in your heart? I was baptized and a regular Catholic church member up to a few years ago. I found out that was going nowhere, remarried a wonderful woman, and started going to her church, where I learned more information about God, Jesus, and the Holy Spirit in one year than I had in a lifetime of being a Catholic. But since I was saved, I have had many more trials and tribulations in my life, and I am not sure what to do when it comes to decision making, which is somewhat confusing. Can you help answer my question?

First of all, it's important to know that your conscience is put there by God. In Romans, Paul makes it clear that all people have the knowledge of God in their hearts, and God has put it there (Romans 1:19). People may try to deny God or deliberately commit sinful acts, but in their conscience they know they are wrong. Of course, someone can sear his or her conscience by repeatedly and willfully denying the truth about God (the Bible calls it "hardening the heart"), but for most people the conscience is a reliable guide for the truth.

The Holy Spirit certainly uses our conscience to bring us to a point of repentance (turning away from sin). In fact, the Holy Spirit must bring us to the point of even desiring God's forgiveness through Jesus Christ. Once we receive Jesus into our lives as Lord and Savior, the Holy Spirit still convicts of sin. Whether you call it the "still, small voice" of the Holy Spirit or your conscience, it's coming from the same source—God.

The other thing you are experiencing is the Holy Spirit enlightening you concerning the truth of God. Before you were a Christian, you were blinded to the truth about God. It probably seemed foolish to you. But once God entered your life through Jesus Christ and now lives in your life through the Holy Spirit, your understanding changed. Paul talks all about this in 1 Corinthians 2:10-16. Read this carefully.

As for your trials and tribulations, they definitely confirm that you are a child of God! Read 1 Peter 4:12-19. This is a very key passage to understand. Trials and tribulations are part of the Christian life, but God will never let you experience more than you can handle, and He promises to get you through them. In fact, when you get through them, you will find yourself stronger and more able to handle future situations. The prophet Jeremiah wrote about this:

*The unfailing love of the LORD never ends! By his
mercies we have been kept from complete destruction.
Great is his faithfulness; his mercies begin afresh
each day. I say to myself, "The LORD is my inheritance; therefore, I will hope in him!"* (Lamenta-
tions 3:22-23).

? Making the right choices can be a struggle
I struggle every day with making the right choices
and being able to give my life completely over to Jesus. I
have to remind myself that I'm not in charge. In one of
your books you say that fear will melt away when you
adopt a heavenly perspective. Mine doesn't seem to be
melting, and I constantly have to work on it. Please write
back.

You asked about struggling with making the right
choices. Well, you're not alone! That's something we all
deal with. Nobody knows the future, and sometimes our
choices aren't cut-and-dried. Life can be frustrating and
confusing at times.

You have hit the nail on the head when you say that the
main problem most of us face is giving our lives completely
over to Jesus. How true! The reason is that we're afraid of
what might happen. We think that we know best, so we
tend to cling to our lives and often leave Jesus out of the picture. The bottom line is that we don't have enough faith to
let Jesus take control.

As we said in the book, the opposite of fear is faith. We
become fearful when we fail to trust Jesus by faith. You
know, there are two kinds of faith. God gives us faith to
trust Him for salvation. This is what Ephesians 2:8-9 talks
about. This is called "primary" faith. It's a once-and-for-all
trusting that God has forgiven our sins through Jesus, and

that by accepting Jesus as our Savior, we will be in heaven forever with Him.

Another kind of faith is ongoing. This is the kind of faith that Ephesians 2:10 talks about. This is the kind of faith that trusts God every day, knowing that He has prepared us to do good things for Him and for others.

When we fear, we are relying on ourselves rather than trusting God with this second kind of faith. At the same time, fear can be a good thing. Fear can be like an alarm, alerting us to a great need that lies ahead of us. When this happens, we need to ask God for the courage to take the next step.

All of us are on the verge of taking the next step. But we can't take that step alone. We need God's courage. The good news is that God promises to give us that courage. Psalm 27:14 says, "Wait patiently for the LORD; be brave and courageous. Yes, wait patiently for the LORD." Jesus said in John 16:33: "Here on earth you will have many trials and sorrows. But take heart, because I have overcome the world."

God will give you courage if you ask Him in faith. And keep at it. Don't give up. God will answer.

May He bless you as you ask Him for courage.

Can we trust our feelings?

I recently started nursing school, and I am completely miserable. I have been praying like crazy for God to help me understand if this is what I am supposed to do with my life. How can I know? What should I do? If I quit school, I will really have nowhere else to go, and everything will go down the drain. How can I override these feelings? Please help me ASAP.

We certainly understand your situation. Trying to figure out if you are doing the right thing isn't easy, especially when it comes to your career.

The fact that you are miserable may or may not have anything to do with whether you are in God's will. We have known a lot of nursing students over the years, and if they have one common denominator, it's that they are all miserable at one time or another—usually at the beginning of the program. Nursing is a tough program. It's not for everyone. The courses are demanding and high-pressure. So just because your stomach is in knots doesn't necessarily mean you aren't doing the right thing.

Usually programs like this are tougher on the front end. Whether it's law school or medical school or nursing school, our experience is that the courses become more manageable as you go along, probably because you build up some experience.

Now, having said that, there is an aspect of your feeling miserable that may mean you need to evaluate whether or not you are in the right program, but we would caution you not to rely on feelings alone. Certainly feelings can help us determine whether or not we are doing what God wants us to do, but on their own, feelings are pretty unreliable. What you want to do is talk with some other people who know you and your situation. Get their advice. No one would be likely to advise you to simply quit school, but they may suggest ways to better deal with the program you are in.

Also, in your time of trial, ask the Lord for strength and wisdom. He cares about you, and He wants to strengthen you. Second Chronicles 16:9 says this: "The eyes of the LORD search the whole earth in order to strengthen those whose hearts are fully committed to him."

You can do it.

How can we find purpose in life?

I just read your book *God Is in the Small Stuff* and really enjoyed it. I gather from this and other books I've

read that God does have a purpose for my life and is
involved in helping me grow, but I'm unsure if that
means a purpose to use my spiritual gifts in church or
actually in every aspect of my life. I would like to turn over
my career to Him also, because this is where I spend the
majority of my day, but I'm unsure how I can actually discover what He wants me to do. I'm ready to do whatever
that is (either more or less money, don't care). Do I give it
my absolute best in my current situation and wait for the
right opportunity to come along when He is ready for me
to move on, or should I constantly search and try different careers? I'm in a very good sales and marketing
position now that gives me access to many contacts, but
I still don't feel as if I'm fulfilling my life's calling. Any
input would be great. Thanks.

You asked about God's purpose for your life. Actually,
you have a very good understanding of what this means. Yes,
God wants us to use our spiritual gifts to serve Him and
others, and this is best done in the local church, where God
can use our gifts to build up others. Also, God wants us to
follow Him in every area of our lives, whether that is at
home or in our vocation.

It's great that you want to turn your career over to Him,
but don't automatically assume that God will take you in
another direction. It may happen, but more than likely God
will use you right where you are. God has given you favor in
your position, and it may very well be that He wants to use
you as salt and light to influence others.

We don't believe you need to search for other careers in
the hope that you will land on something that fulfills your
purpose. As you do excellent work where you are, God will
give you purpose. He may show you new opportunities, but
when that happens, it won't feel forced but very natural
and very much in line with His will for your life.

God's will is more a matter of following Him day by day rather than getting the big picture all at once. The key is for us to make God and His spiritual kingdom the priority in our lives (Matthew 6:33).

With your terrific attitude and perspective, we have no doubt that God is going to use you in significant ways. May He bless you as you follow Him!

❓ How do we handle immature Christians?

I'm in ministry with a group. We have a person on our team who has yet to get out of what I call the infant stage of Christianity. He has cost us a lot of ministry opportunities, but on a personal level I am having trouble telling him that he needs to leave the ministry until he gets his personal issues taken care of.

I've kind of been there myself, and I don't know if keeping him on the team would be a good idea. I talked with a very seasoned Christian just now who is a retired minister, and he suggested that we just go on without him. He was not being mean or malicious, but I seem to know somewhere in my own spirit he's right. There's been a lot of hurt here, and the relationships he has cost us in contacts is just very intense.

I'm past angry and all that stuff, but I really don't know what to do. He has a communication problem and he's called to ministry, but all he can do right now is political activism. Do you have any suggestions? I'm hoping that I'm right, but I feel really aggravated about the whole thing.

If someone feels called to ministry, the call must be verified by others, including someone in a spiritual leadership position, such as a pastor. A call is not in itself a private thing. It must match up with one's character, giftedness (as in spiritual gifts), and the acceptance of other believers (for a good example of being called to ministry, study the conversion experience of the apostle Paul).

A call in itself doesn't mean that the person called is spiritually mature and ready to take on a particular ministry. It may be that some training and discipleship needs to take place (in fact, this is almost a certainty). God is not going to call an immature believer to fill a task that requires maturity.

It sounds like the person in question needs some spiritual maturity, and this may mean he needs to be discipled by another mature believer. If this is the case, then the person who oversees your organization needs to take this person aside and ask him to step down and get some spiritual mentoring before continuing in this particular ministry.

May God give you wisdom as you deal with this.

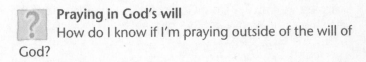

Praying in God's will
How do I know if I'm praying outside of the will of God?

You asked a great question. How do we know if we're praying inside or outside of God's will? One very easy test is this: Is your prayer consistent with what the Bible says? For example, if a Christian were to pray and ask God to bless his upcoming marriage to a non-Christian, that would be praying outside the will of God. The Bible says that a believer should not team up with those who are unbelievers. "How can light live with darkness?" (See 2 Corinthians 6:14.)

You see, anytime we go against what God has instructed us to do in the Bible, we are going against God's will.

Now, we won't find the answers to every situation in the Bible. That's why God's will also involves the wise counsel of other mature believers. If you have a question about whether or not you should do something and you can't find the answer in the Bible, go to another Christian who is mature and trustworthy and get his or her opinion on the situation.

Finally, there's the matter of your own heart. When you pray about something and you don't feel right about it, the Holy Spirit is probably prompting your heart. You have to be careful about responding to feelings that aren't necessarily coming from God, but if you are at a good place with God, then your restlessness or lack of peace may be a solid indicator that what you are about to do isn't in God's will for you.

Why do the wicked prosper?

What is God's definition of justice? How come evil people do not get the consequences of their evil actions and instead have an easier, pleasurable lifestyle? And why is it that Christians often face the consequences of their sins right away? Does God get hurt too when He sees us (the ones He loves most) hurting?

Okay, so you have a few questions there, but they all basically are asking the same thing: Why do the wicked prosper while the righteous suffer?

Guess what? People have been asking this question for as long as evil has been in the world. In fact, King David probably said it best in the Psalms:

> For I envied the proud when I saw them prosper despite their wickedness. They seem to live such a painless life; their bodies are so healthy and strong. They aren't troubled like other people or plagued with problems like everyone else (Psalm 73:3-5).

You'll find verses like that throughout the Psalms. But you will find many more verses that are like this one:

Be still in the presence of the LORD, and wait patiently for him to act. Don't worry about evil people who prosper or fret about their wicked schemes. Stop your anger! Turn from your rage! Do not envy others—it only leads to harm. For the wicked will be destroyed, but those who trust in the LORD will possess the land (Psalm 37:7-9).

As a Christian, your eternal future is secure. You are a coheir with Christ of all that God has. The person who dies without Christ will suffer eternally. So you have to take the long view.

As for God's justice, here's what the Bible says:

He is the Rock, his work is perfect. Everything he does is just and fair. He is a faithful God who does no wrong; how just and upright he is! (Deuteronomy 32:4).

By His nature, God is completely fair and just. He is not responsible for the sin and evil in the world. In fact, sin is an offense to God, and anyone who sins is under God's death penalty. We are all sinners (Romans 3:23), so we face the prospect of eternal spiritual death apart from our faith in Christ (Romans 6:23).

God's justice says that we must pay the penalty for our sins. His love and grace say that Christ has already paid the penalty for our sins on our behalf.

Christians may seem to experience the consequences of their sins right away, but that's because God loves us like a Father (which He is). Would you let your children get by with their sins, or would you love them enough to correct and sometimes punish them? Why would our loving Father do any less for us?

Yes, God hurts when He sees us hurting. He is compassionate. But He loves us too much to let us live in our sins day after day, week after week. The wicked don't know how to live any differently, but as God's children we do.

May God bless you!

Are bad things part of God's will?

I have lost two babies during pregnancy and have struggled greatly with that. I have many questions related to the death of my two precious boys.

Here's one question. Why does God allow a child to be born with birth defects, or to be born so prematurely that death is certain? Is that a part of God's plan? Or did the fall of Adam cause disease and physical imperfection to run amok, and now the cards fall where they may?

There is a verse somewhere in the New Testament that is pretty well-known. Something like "All things work together for the good of those who love Christ." Could that be why one of my babies had spina bifida and the other was born too early to live? For the *good of those who love Christ?* How could something so horrible happening to babies be good for those who love Christ?

I must admit that I struggle with a lot of anger toward God.

I can't rationalize that perhaps God took my babies to heaven early so they could avoid some type of miserable existence here on earth, because there are so many living children who are living a nightmare—abused, hungry, neglected, unloved. That must not be why my babies left this world early.

I do pray about my anger, by the way.

Somewhere in the New Testament Jesus is asked why a man is born blind. He answers that a man is born blind so that God can show His might. The notion that my son may have had birth defects so that God can show His might doesn't sit well with me either. What kind of a loving God would do that?

Maybe I shouldn't be angry at all. Maybe I should be glad that my babies are in heaven instead of going through the struggle of living. Life is good—there's Christmas, and kisses and hugs, kittens and puppies, and all those feel-good things, but there are bad times too.

You can be sure that God never will take offense at your anger toward Him. Many things happen in this world that we do not understand, and perhaps one of the most difficult issues is the one you have had to face twice in your life. Why did those precious ones have to die?

We don't have any answers for you. Yes, we do live in a world of sin and disease and death. No, that was not God's original plan for us and our world, but the price of our having the freedom of choice as a human race included the possibility of choosing to sin, and with that choice came the awful reality of sin's effects on the world.

Yet none of that takes away from God's incredible love for us. In fact, God's love for us is even more amazing in light of humanity's rebellion and opposition to Him.

As for the verse in Romans you quoted, yes, that is hard to understand in light of your circumstances. All we have to fall back on is that God sees the big picture. He is totally sovereign over the universe, and only He knows all things from beginning to end. He cares for us in every detail, and that means He lives with us through our pain. What is the ultimate good in what you are going through? We don't know. But you will know when you stand before Jesus in eternity. Until then, pour out your heart to God as you have been doing. Ask Him for His peace and comfort. Take it one day at a time. And remember that "for the good of those who love Christ" could be a phrase that refers specifically to you, not to other Christians. As hard as it is to imagine, maybe these tragic circumstances will bring you closer to God.

We're sure you have already been reading the Psalms. There you will find a common bond with David, who experienced much and was not afraid to express his anger and frustration with God. Yet he also praised God and put his trust in Him.

You also asked about the man who was born blind. You asked, "Why did Jesus say that the man was blind so that God can show His might?" Actually, the context of this passage is this: Jesus came upon a man who had been born blind since birth. The disciples of Jesus wanted to know why the man was born blind. "Was it a result of his own sins or those of his parents?" (John 9:1-2). "It was not because of his sins or his parents' sins," Jesus answered. "He was born blind so the power of God could be seen in him" (John 9:3). The footnote in the *Life Application Study Bible* may shed some light on this for you:

> A common belief in Jewish culture was that calamity or suffering was the result of some great sin. But Christ used this man's suffering to teach about faith and to glorify God. We live in a fallen world where good behavior is not always rewarded and bad behavior is not always punished. Therefore, innocent people sometimes suffer. If God took suffering away whenever we asked, we would follow him for comfort and convenience, not out of love and devotion. Regardless of the reasons for our suffering, Jesus has the power to help us deal with it. When you suffer from a disease, tragedy, or disability, try not to ask, "Why did this happen to me?" or "What did I do wrong?" Instead, ask God to give you strength for the trial and a clearer perspective on what is happening.

May God bless you and give you His comfort.

Can God read our minds?

My husband says that God cannot read our minds, and God does not know what we might do next. Example: If I am in my car and I get to a stoplight, God does not know if I am going to turn right or left. Is that true?

God knows everything (and that includes knowing things before they happen). He even knows all of our thoughts. This is known as God's *omniscience* (which means He is all-knowing). You and your husband may want to read Psalm 139:1-4 and Proverbs 5:21 (but before you do, make him promise to do some household chores if the Bible proves that he is wrong).

Chapter 13
Morality

In this chapter you'll read about a lot of hot topics every Christian faces. For example, are Christians permitted to drink? What about sex and the Christian? What does God expect of us? And then there are issues of homosexuality, race, and suicide. No question is out of bounds, and we do our best to answer each and every one.

What does the Bible say about drinking?

My brother and I are college students, and we go to different colleges. We both came home for Easter, and it was the first time I had seen him in a while. I was driving with him yesterday, and we were discussing alcohol. A year ago he nearly died of alcohol poisoning because of his initiation into a fraternity. Before I accepted Jesus a couple years ago, I probably should have died on multiple occasions. I have stopped drinking and partying and whatnot, and I now hang out with Christian friends at my university, which means I am never exposed to alcohol. My brother, on the other hand, does not hang out with Christian friends (or at least devout Christian friends). Subsequently, he is exposed to alcohol quite frequently. I really don't know how his relationship with God is, but he says he believes in Him. He also says that the only reason people are restricted from drinking is because of man-made laws, and that's the only reason it's bad at his age (20). He says people drank in the Bible during celebrations, and therefore nothing is wrong with doing it now as long as you don't get drunk.

Basically, I don't really know what to do. I don't know what to say or how to react. I pray for him continually, and I trust that he will eventually fall in love with God, but I don't want it to take a life-altering situation, like a car accident or something super bad, for him to finally come around. Does the Bible discuss drinking or give Christians guidelines on how to handle it? Thank you very much for your help. God bless!

Thanks so much for your e-mail. You are a bright, articulate person, and your concern for your brother is heartfelt. First of all, we praise God for your own journey of faith. How wonderful that you turned your life over to Jesus and are now following Him. Isn't it great to know that your eternal future is secure, and your life here on earth is much more meaningful?

As for your brother, you are absolutely doing the right thing by showing him your concern and compassion. You are identifying with him at his point of need, yet you are not judging him. Continue to show him (and tell him) how much you care for him and that you only want what's best for him. As you have already done, share with him what a difference a personal relationship with God has made in your life. Even though your brother's drinking is a major concern for you, don't necessarily make that the focus of your concern. In reality, your bigger concern is for your brother's eternal soul. His drinking and other behaviors are merely symptoms of someone who is trying to fill the emptiness with a temporary fix. Some people try money and success, and others use socializing and drinking. Someone else may look to some other kind of addictive behavior.

Alcohol abuse is obviously a very big problem among college students, and it doesn't seem to be getting any better. However, your brother seems aware of the biblical teaching on drinking, which is great. Nowhere does the Bible prohibit drinking, but it does very clearly state that we are not to get drunk. See Ephesians 5:18 and notice the context of this verse. It says, "Don't be drunk with wine, because that will ruin your life. Instead, let the Holy Spirit fill and control you." In other words, rather than giving yourself over to the control of alcohol, give yourself over to the control of the Holy Spirit. To read about the contrast between a life given over to our sinful natures and a life given over to the Holy Spirit, read Galatians 5:19-23. Another principle is found in 1 Corinthians 6:19-20, where Paul says that our bodies are temples of the Holy Spirit. We need to honor God with our bodies, not dishonor Him.

Hope this helps you. Again, the best thing you can do is love your brother and pray like crazy! Pray that God will turn his heart around and that He will protect and preserve your brother. You're a good sister. God will bless you for your care and concern.

What does the Bible say about sex?

What does God permit us to do sexually, and with whom? Can you give me Bible verses that explain this? If something is not mentioned in the Bible, is it okay to do? I've been told that I have to "work out my salvation," but

I'm not sure about certain things. I will try asking God, but any ideas would be helpful. Thank you.

Sex is God's gift to us, but the Bible is very specific that the gift is to be used within the confines of marriage. The Old Testament is full of verses about sexual sin. In fact, in Deuteronomy 22:13-30, sex outside of marriage isn't just condemned, it's punishable by death! The New Testament includes no such penalty (boy, that's a relief!), but we are warned about sexual sin (that is, any sex outside of marriage). The apostle Paul writes this in 1 Corinthians 6:18-20:

> Run away from sexual sin! No other sin so clearly affects the body as this one does. For sexual immorality is a sin against your own body. Or don't you know that your body is the temple of the Holy Spirit, who lives in you and was given to you by God? You do not belong to yourself, for God bought you with a high price. So you must honor God with your body.

These sound like old-fashioned values in our culture, don't they? But this is the way God designed sex. As for things not covered in the Bible, we need to use our own good judgment, and in order to fine-tune our judgment, we need to be growing in the knowledge of who God is and what He expects of us. This includes reading and studying the Bible, which "is useful to teach us what is true and to make us realize what is wrong in our lives" (2 Timothy 3:16). Another key component is finding a church where you can learn and grow with other believers. It also means praying and asking God to show you what He wants you to do.

That's where the Holy Spirit comes in. The Holy Spirit is God's presence in you. It's amazing! God dwells in you through His Holy Spirit, and He will speak to your conscience and your will to show you what is right. None of us are perfect, and we all make mistakes, but we should be growing in our attitudes and our actions, becoming the people God wants us to be.

The idea of working out your salvation means that you have a responsibility to do what is right by choosing to grow in your Christian life. God created us with a free will, and we need to use it to choose His ways.

Thanks for your e-mail. God loves you, and so do we!

 ### Should someone who's been unfaithful ever remarry?

I have read all your books and find them so helpful! I have told all my friends to read them all. The reason for this e-mail is that I have an issue. I thought about sending you an e-mail, but then didn't because I decided you would be way too busy to deal with such a basic issue. But as I was discussing this with my mum, she proposed that I e-mail you guys. So here I am! And here's my issue.

I am 21 and have been seeing a guy for about seven months now (before that we were best mates). We have both been brought up in Christian homes, and I think that he has the potential to be the one God has for me (if it's okay to put it like that!). However, he has slept with two others before, and although he's made excuses for them, I still find it hard to forgive. I can't shake the feeling of being third best if and when we get married. I just really need some guidance! Should I not hold against him what happened before? What would God want me to do? I have prayed and prayed about it, that if he isn't the one for me, I would be shown a sign or just be told that he isn't the one I'm meant to be with. But I haven't had anything (not as obviously as I have had with other men anyway). Actually, I am wondering if this issue, and the fact that it bothers me so much, could be a sign of some kind. I'm just really confused by it all! Any help is much appreciated. Thanks!

Thanks so much for your kind words about our books and for reading them! As to your situation with your best mate, you explained it very well, and we think you are really thinking this through before you make a decision that will impact both of you for the rest of your lives. Even though most people these days don't think of marriage in terms of "till death do us part," we think you have the right attitude.

Honestly, we aren't the best ones to give you specific advice in this area because we don't know you or your mate very well. Our advice would be to talk with someone (a pastor or priest) who can give you some relationship guidance. The issue of the past is important because certain patterns and habits, as well as your upbringing, do affect who we are in the present. That doesn't mean we are bound to repeat past mistakes, but we need to deal with the past, which is what you are doing. If you and your mate are getting serious about marriage, then we would suggest some premarital counseling from a qualified person, preferably someone who shares your spiritual convictions (that's why we recommend that you see a pastor or priest).

Having said that, we don't want to leave you completely in the dark on this issue. You asked for advice, so we will give you some! Again, we think you are wise to think about this carefully. You want assurance that the guy you decide to marry will be faithful to you and not fall into any past patterns. Now, none of us can guarantee that we will never repeat past mistakes or commit new ones, but we can ask God to help us, and we can resolve that this won't happen.

Even if you aren't going to marry this guy anytime soon, you don't want to invest your time and emotions in someone who from time to time will feel the need to explore other options. At the same time, you need to give him some latitude. Perhaps these were youthful indiscretions. If he says they were, and if he commits to you that he will remain faithful, then at some point you have to trust him.

Still, you are uneasy about this, aren't you? That could be a natural emotion, or it could be God getting into your conscience (He has a way of doing that). It could be His way of saying, "Be careful here!" Again, we aren't saying that you couldn't have a wonderful life with this guy. But since you have questions, then you need to take the necessary steps to help ease your fears.

May God give you and your mate wisdom as you both seek to do the right thing. A love between a man and a woman is a powerful thing—perhaps the most powerful force in the world. But it is a love that is made even stronger when God is in the picture.

Do blacks and whites see God differently?

Why is it that blacks and whites see God differently? Could it be that whites have used God to oppress, and black slaves saw God as the Great Liberator? Please don't take this offensively because I really do appreciate how you two tackle hard questions concerning religion.

Thanks for your thoughtful question. We think there's a great deal of truth in what you said. Unfortunately, some whites throughout history have used the Scriptures—very badly and incorrectly, by the way—as an excuse to oppress blacks. And your observation that oppressed blacks have seen God as the Great Liberator is very astute. As part of their legacy, slaves left us the great spirituals, which call on God to help and rescue those who have been oppressed.

Having said that, we also need to remember that in both England and in America, many of the leaders of the anti-slavery movements were Christians. William Wilberforce, the great English parliamentarian, was a devout believer. He tirelessly led the fight to abolish slavery, which didn't occur until after his death. And in America, Abraham Lincoln, also a committed Christian, was the great emancipator. We could go on and list many who have fought for freedom for oppressed people through the centuries, and you would discover that many were followers of Jesus Christ.

The oppression of one group of people by another, or of countrymen by a dictator, regardless of their color, is an evil that can only be explained by the sinful condition of the human race. All humanity is in rebellion to God, and unfortunately there will always be those who invoke God's name to justify their evil ways. Those of us who love God and call ourselves Christians should do what we can to oppose oppression and injustice wherever they occur.

Does God make homosexuals the way they are?

How would you reply to homosexuals who say that God made them that way and that they have no choice in the way they are?

The place to start with someone on the issue of homosexuality is God. And it's not just to say, "Well, this is the way God made me." What you have to agree upon is that God exists in the first place. Sometimes people will either accuse God of certain things (such as, "Why would a good and loving God allow evil?"), or they will use God as an excuse (such as, "God made me the way I am"). In either case, they may not believe that God exists at all. They are simply looking for a reason to believe or behave a certain way. What you have to agree on is that God exists as a personal, infinite, holy Being who has revealed Himself to humankind. A good Bible passage to refer to is Romans 1:19-20.

Now, once you agree that God exists, the next question to ask is this: If God exists, wouldn't it be a good idea to find out what He has said about certain things? Here again, you can go to Romans 1. Start with 1:18 and read through verse 27. Tell your friend this is God speaking, not you. Tell him that if it were up to you, you would "live and let live." But what you say doesn't count. It's what God says that counts—that is, if God exists in the first place.

To use the argument "This is the way God made me" seems contradictory. Why would God make someone in a way that went against what He has revealed in His Word? That's the way we would approach it. May God give you wisdom and compassion as you deal with your friend.

Are some sins worse than others?
Is adultery or homosexuality as great a sin as stealing, lying, or murdering?

All sin is an offense to God and makes us guilty before God. But are there degrees of sin? Most theologians agree that while all sin offends God, some sins are worse than others in that they have more harmful consequences in our lives and the lives of others. And some sins bring dishonor to God more than other sins. We're not going to get into the details and start compiling a top-ten list of sins, mainly because God is the final judge of all we do, and it's counterproductive for anyone to judge the sin or action of other individuals. However, each of us is accountable to God for the things we do, both in this life and the next.

? Is suicide the unforgivable sin?

If a person commits suicide, will that person, regardless of his or her faith, go to hell?

Nothing in Scripture supports the position that suicide is an unforgivable sin, or that someone who commits suicide will automatically go to hell. If that were the case, then the Bible would have been specific about it. Jesus made it clear that only one sin is unforgivable, both in this world and the next, and that is blasphemy of the Holy Spirit (Matthew 12:31). To be clear, the Bible does condemn murder, and suicide is a form of murder, but even murder is forgivable.

Interestingly, the Bible gives us accounts of people who didn't want to live. For example, Moses said to God, "I can't carry all these people by myself! The load is too heavy! I'd rather you killed me than treat me like this" (Numbers 11:14-15). Of course, God didn't kill Moses but rather encouraged and strengthened him. This should be a lesson to us. Christians and non-Christians alike who are having thoughts of suicide can be assured that God can help them through that temptation. The Bible gives us this promise:

> *But remember that the temptations that come into your life are no different from what others experience. And God is faithful. He will keep the temptation from becoming so strong that you can't stand up against it. When you are tempted, he will show you a way out so that you will not give in to it* (1 Corinthians 10:13).

? What about masturbation?

I'm a youth pastor and have recently been asked a question regarding masturbation. I teach from the *Jesus Bible*, a New Living Translation by Tyndale, which addresses the issue some, but I would like a bit more advice on how to respond to this issue from a biblical standpoint. I have responded with 2 Timothy 2:22 "Run from anything that stimulates youthful lust," but I feel that I need more practical advice on *how* to run. I know that it all starts with the thought, but explaining that to teenage boys isn't easy. Any help on this most touchy subject would be appreciated.

The issue of masturbation does come up (we've been asked about it more than once). We advise trying to find a middle ground between the old guilt-ridden technique the church used to take (you know, do that and bad things are going to happen) and simply ignoring it. In other words, don't make a big deal of the act itself, but don't ignore it either.

You're certainly on the right track with 2 Timothy 2:2 because masturbation doesn't pop up without some kind of visual or thought stimulation. What we would say is to approach it like any habit that isn't positive. If a young man habitually masturbates, then the habit needs to be broken. But it isn't going to come simply by saying no. A positive new habit must replace the old one. Certainly that starts with the mind. If a guy is always thinking about girls and sex, then masturbation (or sex) is going to be the result. But if a guy thinks about honorable things, then he will get a different kind of result (see Philippians 4:8). Even more, we would suggest guys get involved with something positive, such as the church or a worthy cause. Keep busy. As the missionary William Carey once said, "Do great things for God; expect great things from God."

Do we need to keep the Ten Commandments?

I'm ashamed to admit this, but here goes! I don't follow the Ten Laws and fear that the Lord will judge me for breaking His Ten Laws and cast me to the underworld whether I'm saved or not. It's not a good feeling at all. I just got saved a year ago, and I feel His anger with me, and I still feel the weight of my sins. I did some pretty bad things, such as lying, killing animals for fun, taking money from Mom and Dad, and taking God's name in vain. I've been in and out of jail, and I get angry at God for not taking away my old life before my rebirth. I just feel like God is making me remember those things no matter how hard I try to think about other things. I've tried to be nice to everyone and everything for two years now, yet I still feel guilty. Can you help me?

The Ten Commandments were given to show us that no one can keep God's perfect law. The Bible says that all have sinned and come short of God's perfect standard (Romans 3:23). Yes, you have broken God's law, but so has everyone else. You are not unique, and your sins are not unique. The fact that you feel guilty for your sins means that you don't fully understand what God has truly done for you by forgiving your sins. If you are truly a child of God, He is convicting you, making you aware of your sinful nature. He is asking you to repent. That means to turn away from your sins and turn to God. He has given you a way to get right with Him, and that's through Jesus Christ. Jesus was the only perfect man, and He was able to keep God's law perfectly. Because He was perfect, and because He was God in the flesh, Jesus was able to pay the penalty for your sin by dying on the cross. He put to death all of your sin. The only thing you can do is to accept by faith what Jesus did on the cross for you. You must believe that the death and resurrection of Jesus is enough to forgive you of your sins.

The Bible says that all who believe in Jesus will not die because of their sins but will have eternal life (John 3:16). Jesus didn't come into the world to condemn you but to save you. Short of that, you are going to continue to feel guilty. Talk to your pastor about this. You are carrying a heavy load of guilt that only Jesus can take away.

*C*hapter 14
World Religions and Cults

What makes Christians think they have the one and only true religion? Isn't that an intolerant position? Does it really matter what you believe as long as you're sincere? What about the other major religions in the world, such as Judaism and Islam? How do they measure up to Christianity? In this fascinating chapter, we tackle some of these tough issues related to the Christian faith and other religions.

 How can we know which religion is the right one?

There are so many religions out there. How do you know your religion is the only true way to heaven? What makes your religion the right religion? I don't believe there is one way to heaven. I just believe in a higher being, but I don't believe in any of the multitude of religions out there, so I just try to be a good person.

People generally take two approaches when they sort through all the religions out there. One is to say that all religions are essentially the same, meaning they all eventually point to God. This is a false premise made by people who have never studied religion. Anyone who knows even the basics of religious belief knows that all religions are by definition mutually exclusive. In other words, they contradict each other in basic points of belief and practice. So to say that all are true is illogical. Saying that all religions are false would be better.

The second approach—the one you are taking—is that all religions are false. You are free to do that, but then we would ask if you have investigated the claims of all the religions? How do you know all religions are false? Let's assume for a moment that you have done that and have concluded that no religion is worth following. Our next question is this: Why try to be a good person? What's the motivation? If all religions and belief systems are false, or at least worthless, why should you be a good person? Why not seek all the pleasures you can?

We would answer that the reason you want to be a good person is because something inside compels you to do the best you can. Your desire to live a good life is something you share with every person ever born (except for true sociopaths), which brings us to another question: If all people have some kind of moral framework, where did that inherent morality come from? Did it just evolve, or might God have built that into the fabric of each person? The apostle Paul dealt with this question, and here was his answer:

> *Even when Gentiles, who do not have God's written law, instinctively follow what the law says, they show that in their hearts they know right from wrong. They demonstrate that God's law is written within them, for their own consciences either accuse them or tell them they are doing what is right* (Romans 2:14-15).

? How can you say Christianity is the only true religion?

I read the first 12 pages of your book *World Religions and Cults 101*, and I would have to say I was totally disgusted. You call yourself objective, and yet you have the audacity to say it's possible to discover the one true religion (obviously, you mean Christianity). Who died and made you God? Who are you to claim that all religions except yours are false? And since you guys have no credentials, did you even think of using a qualified editor? You have no business writing a book like this, especially with the ridiculous position you take.

Thanks for your e-mail. We're sorry you were disappointed at what you read in the first 12 pages of our book. Even though it upsets you, logic will tell you that all religions are mutually exclusive. Do you really believe that a devout Muslim believes that all religions are true? How about an orthodox Jew? Do Mormons believe that all religions are the same? Whether you accept it or not, to believe that all belief systems are true is absurd. It's more reasonable to believe they are all false.

Yes, we did use a qualified editor, Dr. Craig Hazen, who received his doctorate in Comparative Religions from the University of California at Santa Barbara. Now we have a question for you. What is your background in studying world religions?

? Does it matter what you believe?

It does not matter what I believe. That is not that the point here. The point is that I am seeking information about religious practices and customs of different religions, not what you believe. I don't want your opinion, just information. You claim that your prejudices will not

affect your objectivity, and then you have the audacity to
ask me to give you my background in studying world religions. That really seems like a waste of time, doesn't it?

Actually what you believe matters a whole lot. What
you believe about God and eternity impacts the way you live
and the way you see things in the world. But that's a
matter for another discussion. The reason we asked you
about your background in studying world religions was
based on your response to our statement, "All religions
can't be true." This is a very logical, reasonable statement
backed by some of the finest scholars and brightest minds
in the field of world religions. Yet you responded by saying,
"Who died and made you God?" From that we had to
assume that you have studied world religions extensively to
conclude that they are all true—if in fact that's what you
believe. Now, we did not deny in our book that all religions
contain truth. But that's different than saying that they are
all true.

We appreciate your honesty in stating that you are
seeking information about religious practices and customs of
different religions. That is a noble goal. However, there is a
nobler and more worthwhile goal, and that's to find out
which of the religions is true. It's fine to search for information, but ultimately shouldn't your search be for truth?

That's all we are trying to do in our book. Unfortunately, we didn't resonate with you, and that's fine. Move on
and find another book that will honestly confront the
truth. Better yet, study the holy books themselves (the
Qur'an, the Talmud, the Book of Mormon, the Bible...) and
read them firsthand to find out which of the holy books
speaks the truth about God, the world the way it really is,
and the human condition—in short, about reality. Merely
knowing about the religions won't help a whole lot if that

knowledge doesn't lead you to the truth about God, the universe, and how you fit into it all. We've enjoyed our dialogue with you. We didn't intend to offend you, but if we've stimulated you to think about these matters more deeply, that's good. May you find the answers and the truth you're looking for.

How is Christianity testable?

I am a sold-out Christian who is reading your *World Religion and Cults 101* book. In it you state that Christianity is a "testable" religion. What tests can be applied? I don't see a direct link to the tests in the text. I am curious because if Christianity is testable and the other religions are not, then we need to be well-versed in this concept.

What we mean by that is that you can test Christianity against objective knowledge, such as history, archeology, and science. The dates, places, names, and events of the Bible are verifiable to a greater degree than any other book of antiquity. And though the Bible is not a scientific book, the statements it makes about the natural world are compatible with what science has discovered. Even more, the statements made about certain phenomena were made thousands of years before science "discovered" them.

Other religions cannot make this claim because their holy books cannot stand up to the scrutiny of history and science.

Is Jesus the only way to God?

If there is no other way to interpret the Christian method of salvation (accepting Jesus Christ as our personal Savior), then do we, as Christians, believe that all others who believe in God but not Christ are destined for hell? Jesus said, "In my Father's house are many rooms." Could He have been referring to rooms for other faiths? Mother Teresa said, "There are many religions and each one has its different ways of following God. I follow Christ. There is only one God and He is God to all; therefore it is important that everyone is seen as equal before God. I've always said we should help a Hindu become a better Hindu, a Muslim become a better Muslim, a Catholic become a better Catholic...." I'm not trying to be coy with my question. I truly do not know and would appreciate your thoughts. Thanks.

Yes, one of Christianity's basic beliefs is that salvation is available through no one else except Jesus. If we believe that the Bible is God's authoritative message to us, that is the only possible interpretation. You quoted Jesus from John 14:2 (NIV) "In my Father's house are many rooms." It's important to read this in context. Right before He said this, Jesus said, "Don't be troubled. You trust God, now trust in me." Clearly Jesus intended His statement about heaven to apply to those who believe in Him. In fact, Jesus is speaking to His disciples, who have already put their trust in Him. He's not talking to the crowds, as He did in other situations. And if you still have any doubts about the intent of Jesus' words about heaven, read John 14:6: "I am the way, the truth, and the life. No one can come to the Father except through me." Not much wiggle room there.

We appreciate Mother Teresa. She was a saint (and may become one literally). But how does helping a Hindu become a better Hindu guarantee salvation? Again, if salvation is only available through Jesus, then how can a Hindu be saved? A Hindu doesn't even believe in the one true God, let alone Jesus. Muslims believe in Allah, but Jesus is merely a prophet, not a Savior. Catholics, of course, believe in Jesus.

The issue that may be troubling you is that Christianity seems narrow and intolerant of other beliefs. Yes, Christianity is narrow in the sense that it is specific about how to be saved. But it is not intolerant. Anyone can be saved. No prequalification is required (or even possible). The same cannot be said for Hinduism or Islam.

God is love, and He doesn't want anyone to perish (2 Peter 3:9). But God has set up a system for salvation based on Jesus, and He has made this very clear. God loved the world so much that He sent Jesus, His only Son, to die in our place, so that anyone who believes in Him will not die but have eternal life (John 3:16).

The questions you are asking are excellent, and we appreciate them very much. May God bless and give you wisdom as you sort these things out.

What does it mean to have right belief?

I was baptized in 1983 as a member of the Worldwide Church of God. I attended services for a decade, and then the church made an astounding turnaround in its belief. Since then I have been spiritually confused. My thought is that if you believe you were not right then, what makes you believe you are right now? I believe there is a God, and Jesus was born and died for my sins, but after that I'm pretty much confused. I mean, how do you know if you should attend a Catholic, Lutheran, Presbyterian, Baptist, or nondenominational church? I think a lot about religion and have talked to others, including my siblings who attend somewhere. I guess after being taught something for so long, nothing else seems right, but then you know what you were doing wasn't right either. Maybe I'm making this too hard, but

I really need some advice or encouragement. Whatever you can offer would be appreciated.

We were very interested to hear from you, knowing what happened with the Worldwide Church of God a few years back. We can certainly understand your confusion over what is right. As we understand it, the bottom line with the WCG turnaround was that the church leadership brought the basic beliefs more in line with the orthodox, historic position of the church, in particular with regard to what it means to be saved. The orthodox (that simply means "correct") position on this is that the only way to be saved is through faith alone in Christ alone. Clearly you understand and embrace this. This is at the core of orthodox Christian belief. The other core beliefs of Christianity are perhaps best stated in the so-called Apostles' Creed, which is as follows:

> I believe in God the Father Almighty; Maker of heaven and earth.
>
> And in Jesus Christ his only Son our Lord; who was conceived by the Holy Spirit, born of the virgin Mary; suffered under Pontius Pilate, was crucified, dead and buried; the third day he rose from the dead; he ascended to heaven; and sitteth at the right hand of God the Father Almighty; from thence he shall come to judge the quick and the dead.
>
> I believe in the Holy Spirit; the holy catholic* church; the communion of saints; the forgiveness of sins; the resurrection of the body; and the life everlasting. Amen.

---

* That is, the true Christian church of all times and all places. This version of the Apostles' Creed is from Wayne Grudem, *Systematic Theology* (Grand Rapids: Zondervan, 1994), 1169.

This creed is called the Apostles' Creed, not because the apostles themselves produced it but because it contains a brief summary of their teachings. In its present form it is dated no later than the fourth century. More than any other Christian creed, it gives us a clear, correct, and concise picture of our faith and what it means to be a Christian.

All of the denominations you listed would embrace this set of beliefs, with the exception of the Catholic Church, which has its own decrees and canons established at the Council of Trent in 1848. For a look at this rather lengthy set of documents, visit: www.history.hanover.edu/early/trent.htm.

What about Roman Catholicism?

I'll get right to the point. What are your thoughts on Catholicism? Popes, bishops, and priests are never mentioned in the Bible, unless I missed it. This makes me wonder if this is a good religion to practice. I'm Presbyterian, and I'm married to a Catholic. I've been reading stuff on Catholics and their beliefs, and I've been attending Mass once in a while (but not participating in the Eucharist). I'm wondering what your opinion is on this religion? Any thoughts and Scriptures you could give me would be appreciated. However, it will be my own decision to continue with this or not. Thanks.

Thanks for your e-mail about Catholicism. We'll do our best to give you some background and a summary of Catholic beliefs. Christianity became the dominate religion of the Roman Empire, but eventually the church was divided into five regions: four in the East and Rome in the West. Because the Roman Catholic Church insisted on maintaining authority over Chrstians everywhere, a major split occurred in 1054 between the Roman Church and the four Eastern regions, creating the Roman Catholic Church in the West and the Orthodox Church in the East. In 1517 Martin Luther "protested" the Catholic practice of selling indulgences (among other things), thereby leading to the Reformation and the formation of the Protestant Church.

All three branches of Christianity have much in common. They are monotheistic (they believe in one God), and they believe that Jesus is the Son of God and the only way to salvation. Where they differ is in the way people relate to God. The Catholic Church teaches that the priest must "mediate" between us and God, whereas the Protestant belief centers on the priesthood of the believer (1 Peter 2:9), meaning that all who put their faith in Jesus Christ—our High Priest—by faith alone have direct access to God (Hebrews 4:14-16).

In addition, the Roman Catholic Church holds these beliefs:

- There are seven sacraments, including baptism, confirmation, penance, and the Eucharist. Regarding the Eucharist, Catholics believe that the bread and wine literally become the blood and body of Christ during Holy Communion (this is called transubstantiation).

- The Catholic Church is the source of complete, divine revelation.

- The authority of the Pope and the bishops of the Church comes directly from Christ. According to Vatican I (1869), when the Pope speaks *ex cathedra* (literally, from his seat of authority), his words bear the same weight as the Scriptures (this is referred to as papal infallibility).

- The Virgin Mary was born sinless (this is known as the Immaculate Conception). Upon her death, Mary was "assumed" in body and soul into heaven (this is known as the Assumption). Catholics stop short of calling Mary the co-redeemer (with Christ) of humankind, but they venerate her above all other saints.

You need to know that not all Catholics or Catholic churches hold to these official positions. In fact, many Catholic churches operate more like Protestant churches than traditional Catholic churches. The key would be whether or not they believe a person is justified through God's grace by faith alone in Christ alone and not by anything we can do to earn our salvation (this is the Protestant position), or through God's grace by faith combined with works (the Catholic position).

So you've got a decision to make. Certainly attending church together with your wife would be important, but you should look at this together. May God bless you and guide you in the process!

 What's going to happen to God's chosen people?
I have been reading *World Religions and Cults 101,* which is fabulous. If I understand the Jewish faith correctly, they do not accept Jesus as God's Son. What does this mean for them as God's chosen people?

Scholars have different views about what is going to happen to God's chosen people in light of Bible prophecy and what God is doing in history right now. Our view is that the Jews are still God's chosen people, but because they rejected Jesus as their Messiah (see John 1:11-12), the good news of

Christ is now available to Jews and Gentiles alike. We believe that God will someday restore His people, but how that will happen is open to speculation. Meanwhile, Jews and Gentiles are alike in that they need a Savior in order to be restored into a right relationship with God. There is no difference with regard to our salvation.

When you have some time, read Romans 9–11 (at the heart of this section is Romans 10:1-4). Here Paul deals with this question, although it's a tough passage to follow. Also, if you're interested in learning about a wonderful ministry to Jews by messianic (that is, "completed") Jews, visit www.jewsforjesus.org.

How can we witness to Muslims?

Hey guys, quick question. I'm a Christian who has been witnessing to a Muslim friend, and I just read your book *World Religions and Cults 101*. In the chapter on Islam, you say that "Allah only loves those he deems to be good" and that he is not personable, merciful, or loving. I've been reading some booklets from a Muslim's point of view that mention verses from the Qur'an that say Allah is most merciful. They also refer to Allah as a "personal God who is close, easily approachable, loving and forgiving." I'm confused! How do I witness to my Muslim friend?

This whole area of Allah and love is very tricky. Yes, the Qur'an will speak of Allah and love, but it's very important that you see the distinction between Allah's love and God's love. Allah loves only those who seek forgiveness and love him. Allah's love is conditional. If you do not love Allah or ask his forgiveness, Allah will not love you or show you mercy. The God of the Bible has a love that is unconditional. "For

God so loved the world," not just those who loved Him in return. "But God showed his great love for us by sending Christ to die for us while we were still sinners" (Romans 5:8).

And here's the tough part for Muslims. They do not know until they stand before Allah in judgment whether or not they have gained Allah's love, mercy, and forgiveness. With the God of the Bible, you know where you stand now because God has clearly revealed what is required for eternal life.

So how do you witness to your friend? First, don't be confused in your own thinking. Know that God loves you and the entire world unconditionally. That should give you tremendous comfort and hope. You don't have to live under the shadow of uncertainty. You don't have to wonder if your works are good enough to satisfy a holy God, because they aren't! Only because of Jesus can any of us stand before God and experience His forgiveness.

Then love your friend, as you already are. Be there to answer her questions honestly. If you don't know the answer, do what you have done and find out as best you can. Ask God to give you a heart for your friend and wisdom to deal with her questions and concerns.

Did Jesus advocate violence?

How does one respond to a member of the Islamic faith who quotes Matthew 10:34-36 and Luke 12:49-53 and says that Jesus did not bring peace to the world but gave rise to a very violent faith?

Let's take up the passages you asked about one at a time. In Matthew 10:34-36, Jesus is referring to the sword metaphorically (the Bible uses many metaphors, as you know). The reason scholars can come to this conclusion is that Jesus later rebuked those who tried to take up the sword to defend him in the garden of Gethsemane (Matthew 26:52). Central to the message and life of Jesus was loving your enemies, not killing them or even getting even with them (Matthew 5:44). So why did Jesus use the metaphor of a sword in this context? The sword is symbolic of God's divine judgment (Psalm 7:12). Here, Jesus uses it as a metaphor of separation between those who believe and those who don't, even if believers and unbelievers are in the same family.

We know that some who follow Christ are hated by their family members. We also know that throughout the centuries, millions have been killed for believing in Jesus. That's what Jesus means when he says He did not come to bring peace, but a sword. The cost of believing in Jesus can be very great. But the love of Jesus must be greater than the love of a family member.

The same comments can be made for Luke 12:49-53. Jesus knew that some would accept His message and some would reject it. In this way His ministry would be like a fire. In the Bible, fire is also a metaphor for judgment and purification. Jesus did come to bring peace—not as the world gives but "peace of mind and heart" (John 14:27).

Muslims and Israel

Why are Muslims so committed to the destruction of Israel?

Regarding Muslims' commitment to Israel's destruction, let's keep in mind that the majority of Muslims don't seem to have those feelings. It's the radical fringe, which unfortunately controls much of the direction of the Islamic faith, who are committed to that end. Unquestionably, animosity has lingered between the Arab nations and Israel since the

Old Testament days. You can see this throughout the history of Israel. No doubt these feelings carry through to the present day, especially since the nation of Israel was formed in 1948, thereby displacing the Palestinians who had been there for centuries. It's a complicated situation that is made worse by the inflammatory statements and policies of radical Muslims. We need to pray for the Middle East and for Israel in particular.

Do Jehovah's Witnesses believe in Jesus?

For the past three years my husband and I have called Jesus our Lord and Savior. That is when we finally found the truth after searching for a long time. We did both Mormon and Jehovah's Witnesses studies in our home for more than a year with each at different times and with different representatives. The reason I am writing you is because I have just read your book *World Religions and Cults 101,* and I have found what I believe to be an error in your chapter on Jehovah's Witnesses. You state that Jehovah's Witnesses "don't consider Jesus to be the Son of God." According to their website, Jehovah's Witnesses do in fact believe that Jesus is God's son. What they don't believe in is the deity of Jesus as we do, that Jesus is God in the flesh.

Even though the Jehovah's Witnesses website makes the claim that Jesus is the Son of God, you need to understand what they mean by that. Actually, it may be easier to explain what the orthodox (that is, correct) doctrine of Jesus Christ is. The orthodox teaching of the church is that Jesus is the only begotten Son of God the Father, equal to God in every way, consubstantial with the Father, meaning that Jesus is of the same substance as the Father. That is what the Scriptures mean when they refer to Jesus as the Son of God.

Jehovah's Witnesses are horrified by that teaching. They believe the Trinity—one God in three Persons (Father, Son, and Holy Spirit)—is a pagan lie. Regarding Jesus, they believe that Jesus and the archangel Michael are the same being. Michael was created first, and then God used him to create all other things in the universe. Jehovah's Witnesses contend that Jesus is a mighty god, but He is not God. He is inferior to the Father because He is created by the Father. So even in the classic definition of sonship, Jesus isn't a son. No son is created by his father.

Furthermore, according to Jehovah's Witnesses, after Jesus died, His humanity was annihilated. He was raised as an immortal spirit who then returned to heaven to become Michael once again. If Jesus is the Son of God, then how can he also be Michael the archangel? It's important that you keep in mind that the Jehovah's Witnesses create confusion by redefining terms and Scripture. Just because they call Jesus the Son of God doesn't mean they hold to what that means.

Is the Word of Faith movement a cult?

I have a question about the Word of Faith movement and those involved. Do you consider the Word of Faith movement a cult? Do the Word of Faith ministers have any affiliation with any Christian denomination?

While we haven't researched this to any great extent, we have been aware of the movement for many years. First of all, we can tell you without a doubt that this is not a cult. By definition, a cult starts with orthodox belief and then strays into heresy by changing the core doctrines. And a cult is usually founded by a single individual who receives new revelation that contradicts the truth of Scripture. As far as we are aware, those in the Word of Faith movement have not done this, and they don't have any one leader.

We also aren't aware that the Word of Faith movement is a denomination, although many of the teachers come from a Pentecostal or Assembly of God background. In any denomination, you are going to find that some people emphasize certain aspects of their Christian experience more than others. For example, some people in the Word of Faith movement place a great emphasis on healing, while others are strictly teachers. If a common thread runs through their teaching, it's the emphasis on the prosperity gospel. In other words, they teach that God wants us healthy, He wants us to prosper, and the way to achieve health and wealth is to have faith.

Our personal belief is that this emphasis is not compatible with the overall teaching of Scripture. It isn't heresy, but it does place the emphasis on rather minor issues. And it may confuse Christians who aren't experiencing those "blessings," causing them to wonder why God isn't more faithful to them. A better approach is to understand that God does not promise to keep us from sickness or poverty or troubles in general, but He does promise to get us through any challenges we may face. If Jesus had to suffer the way He did, what makes us think that we will be exempt? In fact, as Peter explains, our suffering makes us "partners with Christ in his suffering" (1 Peter 4:13).

Will people of other religions be saved?

John 3:16 is the most famous verse of salvation in all of Scripture. How can I interpret that verse to include people of other religions who do not recognize Jesus as the Son of God?

There's no way to interpret that verse in the way you suggest. Christianity is the belief system—the only completely true belief system—centered on the person of Jesus Christ. The Bible clearly explains that there is no other name for people to call on to save them (Acts 4:12). Jesus Himself said, "I am the way, the truth, and the life. No one can come to the Father except through me" (John 14:6). This is not intolerant—it's the truth. There's only one way we are all born physically, and there's only one way we can be born again spiritually.

Chapter 15
End Times

We believe that the lives of Christians and nonbelievers would be significantly different if we knew for certain the exact date and time that the world as we know it will come to an end. But the Bible doesn't give us an exact date and time. It provides many clues, but they are clouded in symbolism. So we are left with many mysteries about the end times. Yet the Bible tells us to expect Christ's return. God evidently wants us to anticipate without demanding specifics. As you'll see from our answers below, we don't even pretend to have answers to all of the questions of when and how the world will end. But we find confidence in knowing that God is in charge and is moving all events according to His plan and timetable.

What is the millennium?
What is the purpose of Jesus' thousand-year reign after the tribulation? What does He plan to accomplish during this time? Will this take place in earth or in heaven?

The thousand-year reign of Christ, known as the millennium, will be a time of ultimate peace on earth with Jesus as King. According to one school of prophecy known as premillennialism, this will take place before all believers from all time are ushered into heaven for eternity.

The saints will reign with Christ during the millennium. People will be born and will die, but they won't be tempted to oppose Christ because Satan will be bound during this time.

Are the rapture and second coming the same?
Are the second coming and the rapture the same thing or two separate events?

The rapture and the second coming are two separate events, although they may occur simultaneously. See 1 Thessalonians 4:15-18.

The word "rapture" means to be "caught up." It describes what will happen when believers, both dead and living, will be caught up to meet Jesus in the air. Depending on the interpretation, this could occur when Jesus comes again (the second coming), or it could be a separate event that precedes the great tribulation.

As far as being prepared goes, we need to "watch and pray." That doesn't mean that we get fixated on the time of Christ's return, but we focus on the fact that He is coming back. No one knows the hour or the day, so we must be ready in our own lives, and we must tell others the good news that God loves them and has provided salvation through Jesus Christ.

What is the order of end times events?
I just read *Knowing the Bible 101* and really enjoyed it. Please help me with one question. You say that we will spend eternity in heaven, which is what I

thought before reading the Bible. As I read Revelation 20, it seems that the thousand-year reign is over, the final judgment has occurred, and Satan and his followers have been thrown into the lake of fire. Chapter 21 then goes on to talk about the new heaven and new earth, and the new city of Jerusalem, and the temple coming down from heaven to the new earth. This seems clear to me. What am I missing?

Your reading of the sequence of events in Revelation 20 and 21 is right on target. One interpretation of these events is that the thousand-year reign is the millennial kingdom, when Christ will reign on earth with all the believers after the second coming. Following the millennium comes the final judgment and then heaven. What may be throwing you off is the description of heaven as the new heaven and new earth, with the new Jerusalem thrown in. All of these are heaven. We talk about this in our book *Bible Prophecy 101*. As we see it, heaven won't be a single location but a variety of places far beyond our capacity to even imagine.

What kind of judgment is waiting for us?
Please explain to me the judgment seat of Christ. I'm hearing that there are five judgments. What are they and how will I be affected?

If you look up the word "judgment" in a concordance, you'll see that it is used in many ways. We discuss judgments more fully in our Bible study *Revelation: Unlocking the Mysteries of the End Times*, but your question really has to do with the two biggies: one for believers and one for unbelievers.

The judgment of believers is called the judgment seat of Christ. This will not be an examination of the Christian's sins. When you receive Christ as your Savior, your sins are forgiven. The judgment seat of Christ will be an examination of our service to God, of how well we handled the talents, resources, gifts, and opportunities God gave us. See 1 Corinthians 3:10-15.

The judgment of unbelievers is called the great white throne judgment. This is for all people who have rejected God's plan of salvation. See John 3:18 and Revelation 20:11-15.

There will also be judgments for the Antichrist, the false prophet, and Satan, and his demons (Revelation 10:9-10). Perhaps this is where you got the idea that there are more judgments.

? Is the European Union evil?

There's something I'm skeptical about believing, yet it's a bit frightening to me. I hear that the EU (European Union) is the revised Roman empire and that the Antichrist will come from that organization. Is that true? And what are the intentions of the EU? Does the Bible speak of a rebuilt Roman empire? And what does the EU have to do with anything? Is it prophesy in action right now?

First of all, when it comes to the future and how it all fits into God's plan for the world, we need to listen to the words of Jesus:

> Don't be troubled. You trust God, now trust in me (John 14:1).

In fact, read John 14:1-4. Jesus was comforting His disciples with the incredible news that He would be going to heaven to prepare a place for them. The same truth applies to us. Yes, things in this world are going to get bad, but all who have put their trust in Jesus have nothing to fear. Jesus has already overcome this world, and He is preparing a place for us in the next.

Second, it's easy to get caught up in world events and try to look for signs behind every movement and every event. Yes, we need to be wise and watch for the Lord's return because we don't know when it will be (Matthew 24:42). But we shouldn't get so caught up in the signs that we miss what Jesus wants us to do every day, and that's to be salt and a light in the place where we are (Matthew 5:13-16).

As for the European Union (EU), it's interesting to note that the EU now contains more than ten nations. About 30 years ago, some prophecy experts were saying that the ten-nation confederacy was going to be a fulfillment of Bible prophecy, but that didn't happen. The prophecy experts also thought that the Soviet Union was going to wage war against Israel, and we know what happened to the Soviet Union. The biggest threat to Israel now is Islam.

As for looking for the Antichrist, people in every generation since Jesus was on earth have been looking for him, and many thought they had identified him (for example, many Christians were convinced that Hitler was the Antichrist).

The point is that no person knows the day or the hour when these things will happen (Matthew 24:36). We need to be aware, we need to be wise, and we need to be ready for the Lord's return. And we need to have a heart for the lost, for they have no hope.

May God give you His peace.

Is Iraq mentioned in Bible prophecy?

My mom heard somewhere that Jeremiah 50–51 seems to prophesy the war in Iraq, saying that God will choose someone to destroy Babylon, which is Iraq on the map. I was wondering if you guys have read that lately and what you think about it. After reading Jeremiah, I don't think that this is World War III.

You are very perceptive! Yes, the prophecy in Jeremiah 50–51 is not dealing with the situation in Iraq, although it does record God's message about the Babylonian empire, which was located in present-day Iraq.

What is interesting, though, is that the Bible uses Babylon as a symbol for evil. God's pronouncement against Babylon in Jeremiah is universal in that God will judge evil once and for all at the end of the age.

God is a gracious God who is being patient so that more people will have a chance to repent (2 Peter 3:9). We know that nothing happens in the world unless God allows it. He directs the governments of the world (Romans 13:1), and He can take them out. In this case, we believe He used America to remove an evil ruler, not unlike the evil Babylonian rulers of ancient days.

What does "this generation" in Matthew 24 mean?

I wonder if you can shed some light on Matthew 24:34, where Jesus says that "this generation will by no means pass away till all these things take place." I can't figure it out. What does it mean? Some people say that "this generation" means the whole race of Jews, but it seems to me that "this generation" means the generation of the 12 disciples.

Great question! Honestly, this verse has been the subject of debate for centuries. The common wisdom from Bible scholars is that the best way to view this verse is to see it in two ways. First, "this generation" refers to the disciples, who are listening to this message of Jesus, usually referred to as the Olivet Discourse (see Matthew 24:1-3). In the immediate context of this passage, "these things" describe the destruction of the Temple in AD 70. In the larger context of the appearing of the Son of Man coming at the end of the age (see verse 30), Jesus is referring to those living at the end of the age. The generation that sees these things will be the generation alive at the second coming.

Chapter 16

Heaven and Hell

What happens when you die? That's one of the biggest questions people have, regardless of what they believe. Is there such a thing as a literal heaven and hell? How can you know you are going to heaven, and why would a loving God send anyone to hell? Why must we be judged, and how is that going to happen? In this chapter we answer those questions, plus one of the most commonly asked questions of all: Will animals—in particular, pets—be in heaven?

Where do people go when they die?

When people die, where do they go? Are people in hell and heaven already?

The Bible is clear that when Christians die, they immediately go into the presence of the Lord (Luke 23:43). Paul wrote that he longed "to go and be with Christ" (Philippians 1:23). However, departed Christians will not receive glorified bodies until the future resurrection at the rapture (1 Thessalonians 4:15-17). This time between a believer's death and resurrection is called the intermediate state. Even though the body has died, the believer's eternal soul exists in a conscious state and enjoys fellowship with God while waiting for a new, resurrected body.

For the non-Christian, it's a different story. A non-Christian who dies also goes to an intermediate state before appearing at the great white throne judgment (Revelation 20:11-15). This intermediate state for the unbeliever is called sheol in the Old Testament and hades in the New Testament. This isn't hell, but it is not a pleasant place to be.

Jesus told a story concerning a rich man and a beggar, both of whom had died. Read it in Luke 16:19-26. You will notice several things about this story that give us a glimpse into this intermediate state that exists for both believers and unbelievers:

- A separation between these two places cannot be crossed.

- Once you are in one place, you can't go to the other.

- Lazarus (the beggar) was in complete comfort.

- The rich man was in agony.

After the intermediate state comes a time of final judgment. Again, there is a difference between the place believers go (heaven) and the place unbelievers go (hell). Both are real places, and both are eternal. To see the difference between the two, read Revelation 20:11-15 (hell) and Revelation 21:1-4 (heaven).

Is hell for real?
What is hell like? Is it for real? Why would God send me there?

Great questions! Too many people don't take hell seriously, including many Christians who wonder if hell is more symbolic than real. So what's the deal? Is hell for real? In a word, yes. The Bible uses a variety of images to describe hell:

- a place of outer darkness (Matthew 8:12)

- a furnace (Matthew 13:42)

- a place where there will be weeping and gnashing of teeth (Matthew 13:42)

- eternal fire (Matthew 25:41)

- a place of terrible punishment (Matthew 25:46)

If you were to look these references up, you would notice something very interesting. Jesus is the one who gives each of these descriptions. In fact, most of the teaching about hell in the Bible comes from Jesus. Why would Jesus go into such detail? Perhaps because He doesn't want us to go there.

Now, some people would say that these descriptions are simply images, that Jesus is speaking in parables as He so often does. Okay, let's say that hell won't exactly be a furnace (Matthew 25:41), a lake of fire (Revelation 21:8), or a bottomless pit (Revelation 9:1-2). Let's say these are symbolic of hell. Does that make it any better? We don't think so. If anything, it may make it worse, because the reality of something is usually more intense than the symbol. As the theologian R.C. Sproul suggests, "The function of symbols is to point beyond themselves to a higher or more intense state of actuality than the symbol itself can contain." Well, when it comes to hell, that can't be good.

As for why God would send you to hell, we need to clarify just exactly what that means. To say that God sends anyone to hell implies that God is doing something *to* us, like a parent who sends a child to his room (only a lot worse). The truth is that the human race, because of sin, *deserves* to be in hell already. We have rebelled against God and fallen far short of His perfect standard (Romans 3:23). Consequently, under the system God set up in the Garden of Eden, the penalty for this sin is death (Genesis 2:15-17).

We know that it's difficult to comprehend how a loving, merciful God could allow people to die in their sins and live in hell forever, but we need to realize that God is also holy and just. He can't let sin go unpunished. At the same time, God isn't willing that any of us should die and go to hell, so He is patiently giving us more time to turn back to Him (2 Peter 3:9). But someday God's patience will run out, and He will judge humankind (2 Peter 3:10).

That's the bad news. The good news is that God loves us and has given us a way to avoid hell, and that's Jesus. In the most famous verse of the Bible, Jesus Himself tells us how this works:

> *For God so loved the world that he gave his only Son, so that everyone who believes in him will not perish but have eternal life. God did not send his Son into the world to condemn it, but to save it* (John 3:16-17).

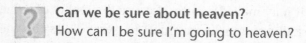 **Can we be sure about heaven?**
How can I be sure I'm going to heaven?

You can be sure you will go to heaven. Absolutely. Get a Bible and look up the verses we are going to give you. First, you must receive Jesus Christ as your personal Savior. This means believing that you are a sinner who has offended a holy God and needs to be saved. You cannot save yourself. You must receive Jesus through faith. See John 1:12; Romans 10:9-10; and Ephesians 2:8-9.

Once you receive Christ, you are guaranteed to go to

heaven. See John 3:16; 5:24; and 14:1-6. You won't always feel saved. But you need to know that salvation is a fact, not a feeling. See Romans 8:38-39; Philippians 1:6; and 1 John 5:13.

Is it okay to talk to our departed loved ones?

My mother died recently after a long illness. I went to see her every day at the nursing home, and I am dealing with the grieving process now. I know her soul is with Jesus. I want to know if it is a sin for me to talk to her. I find as I am going through her things, I will say things to her: "Gee, Mom, thanks for saving this or that. I remember the good times we had then." Or when I visit the grave, I might say, "Hello, Mom, I brought your favorite flowers. I miss you a lot. It's a pretty day today. Sissy says she will come to see your grave this summer—you know how she is." I don't expect an answer, and I'm not trying to conjure up some kind of weird sighting of her or anything like that, but am I sinning to talk to her? I know the Bible says for us not to try and communicate with the dead. I'm not trying to make her appear or anything, it's just that I miss talking to her. I would never do séance or any of that weird stuff, but is it okay for me to talk to her, or is that a sin? Should I just be talking to the Lord about her and stop talking to her? I don't do it every day, just every once in a while when I am feeling very sad. Thank you for the answer.

Thanks so much for your e-mail. We appreciate your writing to share your story.

First of all, may we express our deepest condolences on the loss of your mother. We pray for God's comfort and peace for you and others in your family. Losing a loved one is never easy, especially someone so close.

Second, we want to assure you that you are not sinning by talking to your mother. When the Scriptures warn us about communicating with the dead, it is in the context of using a medium to conjure up the spirit for the purposes of communication. What you are doing is simply honoring her memory by expressing your feelings and gratitude.

The Bible is also clear that when we pray, we are to pray to God alone, not to the departed. Again, you aren't praying to your mother (like someone might pray to Mother Mary). You are simply acknowledging the impact she had in your life. Can your mother hear you? The Bible isn't clear on this matter. Certainly there is an indication that the departed saints are watching us (see Hebrews 12:1), but whether individual departed saints can hear individuals is unclear. What we do know for sure is that your mother is safe in the arms of Jesus. She is experiencing the most wonderful, indescribable life possible. You can praise God for that. Meanwhile, God will take care of you if you continue to put your trust in Him.

Will there be animals in heaven?
Someone told my daughter that no animals will be in heaven, and she was a little upset. I tried to reassure her, but I didn't have any Scripture to support it. What does the Bible say about this?

Thanks for your question. Actually, it's one of the most common questions we get, and we don't have an easy answer. Since the Bible doesn't speak directly to this issue, about the best you can do is to find out what the Bible scholars say about it. Some don't think animals will be in heaven because the Bible is silent about the subject. But others, such as Peter Kreeft, who has written extensively about heaven, think it's a real possibility. Kreeft says that other nonhuman things will be in heaven (such as green fields and flowers), so why not animals? "Animals belong in the 'new earth' as much as trees," he writes.

Dr. Kreeft makes the point that human beings were meant, from the beginning, to have stewardship over the animals (Genesis 1:28). Since the human race has violated that divine directive on earth now, it's reasonable to believe that God will make that relationship right in heaven. Whether or not our own pets will be in heaven is another question. In order for that to happen, they would have to be resurrected and given glorified bodies like those human beings who have put their trust in Christ. Animals do have souls—the soul is what gives all living creatures life—but their souls are not eternal. Only those beings created in the image of God have eternal souls, and the Bible is clear that human beings are the only beings created in God's image (Genesis 1:26-27).

Can sin separate us from God?

My precious daughter has loved and served the Lord Jesus Christ for most of her twenty-three years, but she has backslidden over the last three years. She tells me she no longer thinks that Jesus Christ is the only way, and she is no longer even sure about the claims made by Him or Christians on His behalf. She now lives in sin with a nonbeliever, and this has absolutely shocked me and her church family. My question is this: If she were to die now (God forbid), would she go to hell?

Our heart goes out to you. We each have two grown children, and we know how important it is to see our children walk with the Lord. When that isn't the case—especially when sons or daughters are confused about their beliefs—it can be a heartache. But it isn't the end of the world. There is hope.

First of all, if your daughter has truly given her life to Christ, then nothing can take her salvation from her. The Scriptures tell us this is true:

> *And I am convinced that nothing can ever separate us from his love. Death can't, and life can't. The angels can't, and the demons can't. Our fears for today, our worries about tomorrow, and even the powers of hell can't keep God's love away* (Romans 8:38).

God is the one who saves us, not us (Ephesians 2:8-9). Because God is the one who saves, God will keep us saved.

Now, about your daughter's current situation. She reminds us of the prodigal son (or in her case, the prodigal daughter). She has chosen to walk away from her heavenly Father, but her heavenly Father hasn't walked away from her. She is an adult who has formed her own opinions about what she wants to do and what she wants to believe, so the best you can do is continue to love her and pray for her (as you are no doubt doing). Don't condemn or judge her for straying from the Lord. Simply communicate your love and your own firm belief in the God who loves you and your daughter so very much.

And remember, the prodigal son returned to his father, who threw a banquet in honor of the son who was once lost but was now found. May God bless you, and may your daughter sense the love of God like never before.

? God and hell

Why does God allow someone to be born if He knows before that person is born that the person will go to hell?

That's a very good question with no easy answer. Perhaps the best way to look at it is that even though God knows everything about us, including the decisions we are going to make, He doesn't predetermine those choices. God created human beings with a free will so that they could willingly choose or reject Him. The alternative would be to create us as robots who would have no choice in the matter. Having free will, of course, means that we have the freedom to reject God and therefore pay the penalty for that rejection, which as you say is eternal separation.

So why does God allow someone to be born, knowing that person is going to reject Him? Like we said, even though God knows, the decision is still up to each individual. The alternative is that no person would be born. In other words, the alternative to living with the possibility of choosing or rejecting God is to not live at all.

Hope we've been able to stimulate your thinking on this matter. Keep thinking, and keep seeking God!

Are there three hells?

Are there three hells? I learned that when a person dies the body goes to hell when it is buried. The second hell is the place of the departed spirit. And the third hell is the lake of fire. Is this all correct, or are they all just the same thing with different names?

The King James Version of the Bible uses three different words for hell:

- Sheol (used 31 times in the Old Testament), which was the place where both the ungodly and the godly go at death. The word is used most often in the Wisdom literature (Psalm 139:8 is an example).

- Hades (used 10 times in the New Testament), is the New Testament counterpart of sheol. It's where all of the dead dwell.

- Hell (used 11 times in the New Testament), also "Gehanna," referring to the place of punishment of the ungodly. This name coincides with our understanding of hell as it is usually used.

Few people take hell seriously, but it is very real, and it is worse than we could ever imagine. In Matthew 25, Jesus talked about outer darkness and "eternal punishment" (verses 30,46). In a parable (Matthew 13:37-42), Jesus taught that hell is a place of eternal torment and punishment waiting for those who reject Him. As for having bodies in hell, the Bible isn't specific, but it is clear that there will be eternal conscious punishment.

 ### How can we be sure someone will be in heaven?

I'm 35 years old, and I'm writing from rainy England. I became a Christian after the death of my father. He succumbed to cancer in 1998, yet I didn't accept the Lord until 2002. If all goes to plan, I intend to spend eternity with God in heaven. As far as I am aware, my father was not a believer—although I might be wrong. Is there *any* chance that I will see my father again in heaven? Is it right to ask if this is a possibility, or should I concentrate more in making sure I live a godly life here on earth? My wife is not yet a believer, which is a concern for me, and I would like my two daughters to know about God (I'm not sure my wife appreciates this). With Jesus, my life feels complete. Sure, I've got loads to learn and even more things to correct. But I've got my wife, my girls, my business, my house, and my health. My desire is to constantly praise God for giving me all of this! Yet I am concerned for my family. I would appreciate your thoughts on this. Thanks for your help.

Thanks for your e-mail. It's always nice to hear from readers "across the pond." We appreciate your candor and your question about your father and your family. It's truly from your heart! Regarding your father, you must always be hopeful that he was a believer. If he was—and only God knows the truth about his situation—you will see him in heaven. That's the hope you must live with.

It won't do you any good to dwell on his situation. You could drive yourself crazy thinking about it. As you said, you need to concentrate on living a life that pleases God. Read Ephesians 2:8-10. This tells us that God saves us by His grace, and He does it so we can do the good things He planned for us long ago. Concentrate on your own family. Don't preach at them or try to persuade them by your words only. The life you live before God, loving Him and loving others, will be a testimony to your own wife and your two daughters. What will happen is that they will ask you questions about your growing faith, and you should be ready to respond with gentleness and respect (1 Peter 3:15-16). Study the Scriptures and learn all you can about God (Colossians 1:9-10). As you grow, your life will become a beautiful fragrance to them (2 Corinthians 2:14).

We love the way you said it: "With Jesus, my life feels complete." That's absolutely right! It doesn't mean that everything in your life will go the way you want it, but God has blessed you, and He will continue to bless you. Thank Him for your blessings and continue to pray for your family. They will come around in God's good time.

The Bible and reincarnation
What does the Bible say about reincarnation?

The Bible doesn't actually mention reincarnation, but it does tell us what happens when we die:

> *And just as it is destined that each person dies only*
> *once and after that comes judgment, so also Christ*
> *died only once as a sacrifice to take away the sins of*
> *many people* (Hebrews 9:27-28).

Clearly reincarnation is incompatible with Scripture.

The security of heaven

Thank you for your answer. Lately I have heard too many "Christians" discussing the issue of reincarnation with no solid information to back it up. I have heard the subject discussed on Christian TV, and there always seems to be a big question mark remaining for the viewer. When I reach my final destination in the kingdom of God, that is where I want to remain. No returning for me, no matter how much I am enjoying my earthly journey. Thank you again.

We're glad we helped settle your mind on this issue. Yes, it would be rather distressing for a Christian to wonder if your final resting place is secure. You've got a great attitude. We appreciate you!

Does everyone have to die?

I have a question about Enoch and Elijah. These men were the only ones to go to heaven without dying. Does the Bible say anything about us walking and talking with God and having that hope that we won't die like these men? I understand when Jesus Christ our Lord comes, we will be taken without dying, but can anyone be so righteous that they will be taken earlier because God doesn't want to see them die? I grew up hearing about Enoch and wanting to be like him, yet it is so hard to be righteous in this evil world. Thanks for helping me out.

Interesting question about being taken to heaven without dying. You're exactly right that Enoch and Elijah are the only men who were "translated" to heaven without dying. Jesus was taken into heaven, of course, but first He had died and been resurrected. Are there any such occurrences today? We don't know of any documented cases, but it would not be outside the realm of possibility because God can do anything!

There are certainly plenty of cases of mysterious disappearances where people are assumed to have died even though no body was found, but we don't know of exceptionally godly people who never had to die. We do know of plenty of godly people who died before their time, and you do too. Sometimes they are children, and other times they are adults who had their whole lives in front of them. Sometimes you wonder if God "takes" certain individuals in order to spare them pain or because they are so special that they deserve to live in heaven with God more than on earth with us. There's a verse in Isaiah that seems to confirm this:

> *The righteous pass away; the godly often die before their time. And no one seems to care or wonder why. No one seems to understand that God is protecting them from the evil to come. For the godly who die will rest in peace* (Isaiah 57:1-2).

As for the rest of us mere mortals, yes, we live in an evil world, and sometimes we long for the peace and perfection of heaven. If you're having such thoughts, it simply means you know that a better place awaits you. C.S. Lewis once wrote, "If I find in myself a desire which no experience in this world can satisfy, the most probable explanation is that I was made for another world."

Meanwhile, Jesus told His disciples that in this life they would face many "trials and sorrows." And then He told them, "But take heart, because I have overcome the world"

(John 16:33). We need to claim the promise of Jesus as we live in this evil world. We may be privileged to be caught up in the air alive with Jesus when He comes again, but it will be no less a privilege to be resurrected from the dead. In fact, the Bible tells us that when Jesus returns for His own, the dead in Christ will rise first (1 Thessalonians 4:15-18). It's a powerful promise, one that should encourage and comfort you.

Why must we be judged?

If God throws our sins into the "sea of forgetfulness" once we become saved, why do we still have to stand in judgment with them before God?

There are two kinds of judgments waiting for all humanity. One, the great white throne judgment, is for those whose names are not written in the book of life (see Revelation 20:11-15). All those who have rejected God's plan of salvation through Jesus Christ will be subjected to this judgment.

The other judgment is the judgment seat of Christ. This is where all believers will stand before Christ to be judged for the deeds they have done (Romans 14:10-12; 2 Corinthians 5:10). Only those things done for Christ will last. This is not a judgment to see who gets into heaven but to reward believers for the good things they have done.

If you have asked Jesus Christ to forgive you and you have received Him as your Savior and Lord, your sins are forgiven once and for all. As a Christian, you will not be judged for your sins because Jesus dealt with those on the cross. However, you will stand before Jesus to account for the things you did. Why? In order to receive your rewards. The apostle Paul writes that there will be degrees of reward for believers (see 1 Corinthians 3:12-15). However, we want to be very clear. The joy of each person in heaven will be overflowing for all of eternity. We won't look at those with greater rewards as being better off than we are. There will not be degrees of happiness. Every person will be completely and utterly fulfilled.

Still, we are encouraged in Scripture to work for the Lord in such a way that He will be pleased when we see Him face-to-face. Here is how the writer of Hebrews put it:

> *Think of ways to encourage one another to out-bursts of love and good deeds. And let us not neglect our meeting together, as some people do, but encourage and warn each other, especially now that the day of his coming back again is drawing near* (Hebrews 10:24-25).

The Bible and heaven

I'm going to freak you out by saying that I am a Christian who doesn't plan on going to heaven and doesn't want to. Why would I want to go to heaven when God will be here on the new earth? Revelation 21:1-3 says that God will dwell with man on earth in the new Jerusalem. And according to Matthew 5:5 and Psalm 37:11, the meek shall inherit the earth, not go to heaven. The only people going to heaven are 144,000 Jews of His choosing. I'd like an answer because most people think it isn't worth their time to try to convince me otherwise, or they don't know more than they have been told and choose to believe what man says over the Word of God.

It sounds like you've been talking to some Jehovah's Witnesses! Despite what you have heard, the evidence for heaven in the Scriptures is clear. The Lord says, "Heaven is my throne" (Isaiah 66:1). We are taught to pray, "Our Father in heaven" (Matthew 6:9). Jesus has gone to heaven and is now at the right hand of God (1 Peter 3:22). Jesus said that He is preparing a place for us in heaven (John 14:1-4).

When Stephen was in the process of being stoned to death, he looked up into heaven and saw Jesus standing at the right hand of God (Acts 7:55-56). Heaven is a real place with real characteristics. If all those who believe in Jesus were not going there, why would the Scriptures describe it in such detail?

Now, you mention the new earth, and that is definitely a part of heaven, not separate from it. Scripture often talks about new heavens and a new earth (Isaiah 65:17; 66:22) as well as a new heaven and a new earth (2 Peter 3:13 [NIV]; Revelation 21:1). What this means is that in addition to a renewed heaven, God will make a new earth. Not only that, but there will be a new Jerusalem, "coming down from God out of heaven like a beautiful bride prepared for her husband" (Revelation 21:2). All of these—the new heaven, the new earth, and the new Jerusalem—are part of heaven. And there won't be just 144,000 Jews in heaven. Revelation 7 indicates that the 144,000 Jews (12,000 from each of the 12 tribes of Israel) will become Christians and spread the message of Jesus Christ around the world during the tribulation.

Heaven will be a glorious place far beyond what any of us can even imagine. God dwells in heaven now, and when everything is ready, Jesus will come for His own (John 14:3) so that we may live forever with Him, basking in the glory of God and the Lamb (Revelation 22:3).

A Closing Note

We had to end this book somewhere, and we figured heaven was a pretty good place to stop. At the same time, this book feels somewhat unfinished. Perhaps that's because we barely scratched the surface of possible questions about God and the Christian life. True, we answered a bunch of questions—and we hope we covered some of yours—but we know you can probably think of a bunch more.

Having so many questions about God isn't a bad thing. It doesn't mean that He's like the man behind the curtain in the *Wizard of Oz*, using smoke and mirrors and lots of noise to throw us off. No, the reason God prompts so many questions is that He is so far beyond us in every way. You could spend a lifetime trying your best to get to know Him (and we hope you do), and you would still have much to learn.

The good news is that if you have a personal relationship with God through Jesus Christ, you will have eternity to learn about Him. Meanwhile, God has given you all you need to personally know and experience His love, His grace, His faithfulness, and so much more. God may be beyond knowing completely, but He is not beyond knowing. So continue to ask your questions, and continue to seek answers. And may God bless you every step of the way.

Index

Scripture Index

Bruce and Stan
would enjoy hearing from you!

mail
Twelve Two Media
P.O. Box 25997
Fresno, CA 93729

e-mail
info@christianity101online.com

website
www.christianity101online.com

When you visit the Christianity 101® website, you will find a variety of resources to help you in your own study of the Christian faith and the Bible, including...

- *Books and Bible Studies*—The Christianity 101® series includes more than a dozen books that cover most of the important issues addressed in this book, only in more detail. You will also find books on a wide variety of subjects ranging from personal relationships to the sovereignty of God.

- *Current Issues*—From time to time Bruce and Stan will post articles about some of the most pressing cultural issues of our day. You will also find informed opinions from some of today's most thoughtful Christians.

- *Daily Devotion*—Each day will feature a timely devotion to help you put your life and your daily circumstances into God's eternal perspective.

- *Answers to Your Questions*—Do you have a question about something not covered in this book? Do you want to dig deeper into a particular issue? Ask your question and you will get a response.

Christianity 101® Studies

Now That You're a Christian

If you're a new believer, you'll connect with these honest, encouraging responses to questions that new Christians often have. You'll discover what God has done for humanity, how you can know Him better, and how you can reflect the love of Christ to people around you.

Bible Prophecy 101

In their contemporary, down-to-earth way, Bruce and Stan present the Bible's answers to your end-times questions. You will appreciate their helpful explanations of the rapture, the tribulation, the millennium, Christ's second coming, and other important topics.

Creation & Evolution 101

In their distinctive, easy-to-access style, Bruce and Stan explore the essentials of creation and evolution and offer fascinating evidence of God's hand at work. Perfect for individual or group use.

Knowing the Bible 101

Enrich your interaction with Scripture with this user-friendly guide, which shows you the Bible's story line and how each book fits into the whole. Learn about the Bible's themes, terms, and culture, and find out how you can apply the truths of every book of the Bible to your own life.

Knowing God 101

Whatever your background, you will be inspired by these helpful descriptions of God's nature, personality, and activities. You will also find straightforward responses to the essential questions about God.

Bible Answers 101

Using hundreds of questions from readers, Bruce and Stan tackle some of the biggest issues about life and living the Christian faith, including, *What happens when we die? Is Christ the only way to salvation? How can we know there is a God? Is the Bible true?*

Growing as a Christian 101

In this fresh look at the essentials of the Christian walk, Bruce and Stan offer you the encouragement you need to continue making steady progress in your spiritual life.

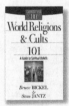

World Religions and Cults 101

This study features key teachings of each religion, quick-glance belief charts, biographies of leaders, and study questions. You will discover the characteristics of cults and how each religion compares to Christianity.

Evidence for Faith 101

Bruce and Stan present Christian apologetics without polemics and without clichés as they tackle vital questions people of all ages and beliefs are asking. Exmine evidence—from history, from the lives of people changed by faith, and from our world—as you form and under-stand your convictions about God.

Christianity 101® Bible Studies

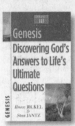

Genesis: Discovering God's Answers to Life's Ultimate Questions

"In the beginning" says it all. Genesis sets the stage for the drama of human history. This guide gives you a good start and makes sure you don't get lost along the way.

Galatians: Walking in God's Grace

With their trademark humor, deep respect for the authority of Scripture, and penetrating insights into current trends, Bruce and Stan reveal the serious problems Paul addressed and practical solutions he provided. They show that his presentation of God's grace speaks as forcefully today as it did to his original readers.

John: Encountering Christ in a Life-Changing Way

This study reveals who Jesus is by demonstrating the dramatic changes He made in the lives of the people He met, including Nicodemus, the woman at the well, Lazarus, and John, "the disciple whom Jesus loved."

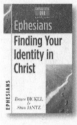

Ephesians: Finding Your Identity in Christ

Verse for verse, the book of Ephesians is one of the most profound, powerful, and practical books in the Bible. This guide reveals the heart of Paul's teaching on who believers are in Christ.

Acts: Living in the Power of the Holy Spirit

Bruce and Stan offer a straightforward look at the ongoing ministry of Jesus through the church. They highlight the drama of the early Christians' triumph over darkness and their explosive growth from a band of 120 fearful followers to a thriving, worldwide church.

Philippians/Colossians: Experiencing the Joy of Knowing Christ

This new 13-week study of two of Paul's most intimate letters will inspire you to know Christ more intimately and maintain your passion and vision. Filled with helpful background information, up-to-date applications, and penetrating, open-ended questions.

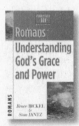

Romans: Understanding God's Grace and Power

Paul's letter to the church in Rome is his clearest explanation and application of the good news. This fresh study of Romans assures you that the Gospel is God's answer to every human need.

James: Working Out Your Faith

Bruce and Stan show that the New Testament book of James is bursting with no-nonsense help to help you grow in practical ways, such as perceiving God's will, maintaining a proper perspective on wealth and poverty, and demonstrating true wisdom in your speech and actions.

1 & 2 Corinthians: Finding Your Unique Place in God's Plan

This enlightening study explores the apostle Paul's helpful responses to issues that churches continue to face today: maintaining unity in the church, exercising spiritual gifts, and identifying authentic Christian ministry.

Revelation: Unlocking the Mysteries of the End Times

Have you ever read the final chapters of the Scriptures, only to finish with more questions than answers? Bruce and Stan help you understand Revelation's encouraging message and apply it to your life today.